Swingers AND Crooners

Swingers AND

LESLIE GOURSE

Crooners

The Art of Jazz Singing

Franklin Watts

A Division of Grolier Publishing
New York / London / Hong Kong / Sydney
Danbury, Connecticut

Swingers and Crooners

Jazz singing, which was created in America, isn't really very old. It developed from other styles of music—primarily the gospel and the blues of African-Americans—in the early days of the twentieth century. The roots of jazz go back even further. African-Americans had brought their drum rhythms and singing traditions from Africa. As slaves until 1863, they were forbidden to play drums. So they sang messages to each other in the fields and other workplaces. None of the men were permitted to learn to read and write. A man could be executed if he became literate. But slaves could meet at night and sing together.

African-Americans formed their own Christian churches. Many became Baptists and Methodists, singing gospel songs and spirituals, sometimes with words and melodies of their own invention. Or they used hymns written by nineteenth-century composers of religious music. Whatever African-Americans sang, they often embellished melodies, rhythms, and harmonies beautifully and imaginatively.

After the Civil War and the end of slavery, African-Americans stayed faithful to gospel and spirituals. The songs celebrated their fervent belief in total redemption and eternal life—the hope that one day they would be free of racial persecution on this earth, when they rose to meet the Lord. In churches, people with the most beautiful voices and the greatest ability to encourage others in faith received great respect.

African-American churches flourished, especially in the twentieth century. Segregation played a role in this growth. In the South during the 1890s, states passed laws separating the races in almost all aspects of their lives, from schools to railroad waiting rooms. Everything was separate—and unequal. On Sundays, African-Americans sang and prayed in their churches to give themselves courage to rise above hardships. A new church was founded. Called by several names—the Sanctified Church, the Pentecostal Church, and the Church of Holy Rollers—it gave believers a chance to express their faith more exuberantly than ever. They outshouted, outsang, and overwhelmed their troubles. The rhythms of their songs grew so exciting, as services pro-

10

gressed, that people were often swept up into emotional frenzies. They shook, shrieked, and fainted.

Strict, conservative Christians did not want their children to go to Sanctified Church services, which were seen as overly emotional and included some activities that reminded people of African ceremonies. But people of all faiths were intrigued by the free-spirited, rocking, swinging shouts and cries of the Sanctified churchgoers. Singers in all the churches added at least a little of the feeling of Sanctified music to their own services to express themselves more profoundly. While they were in church, they knew, nobody would persecute them.

Many African-Americans lived totally church-centered lives. But others took church melodies, changed the words, and sang about their unhappy love lives, poverty, lonesomeness, struggles with bad habits, racial persecution, faithless friends, and even good times—all of life's experiences. They called their songs the blues. Whether they were sad or humorous, the songs could be melodious and haunting. The blues were simple in form; they could have twelve, sixteen, or thirty-two bars, and they could be slow and mournful with long lines (called the long meter), or driven by short, fast lines (called the short meter). White people appreciated the blues, too. Everyone had the blues at one time or another. So white blues singers became adept at imitating African-American singers.

To create both gospel music and the blues, African-Americans had blended their own African-derived rhythms with the European harmonies popular with whites. To this mixture African-Americans added their genius for improvisation. They improvised because they saw no sense in going directly from one note to another, the way the music was written. So singers (and instrumentalists, too) glided between the notes, adding notes and tones that had never been written for the songs. The more creative the singer, the more powerfully expressive the music.

Singers also used traditional African call-and-response techniques. That is, in church, when a preacher called out a line, the congregation repeated and embellished it. That's how people encouraged themselves to reach new heights of ecstasy. They might improvise such simple words as "Yes, Lord," or they might hum to imply words expressing emotional pain or joy. They might sing long, completely new lines. The style of their embellishments made their music impassioned. Blues singers did the same thing. Through singing, they changed their daily misery into the joy of enduring creativity. The songs gave them control over their lives and established their individuality.

Blues singers usually accompanied themselves on guitar. Some also played banjos, ukuleles, harmonicas, or homemade instruments such as one-stringed bass fiddles, glass jugs, tin cans, and washboards. But the best-known blues singers usually played guitar or hired accompanists who played piano or guitar.

Some blues singers worked in the countryside and in small towns. They sang stories about the lives of rural African-Americans. Others performed on city street corners or in clubs or joints known as honky-tonks, where liquor was served. Most country and small-town blues singers lived in the South. Some became famous in their regions for their original songs and characteristic styles. Some gained notoriety for their lives, too. Huddie Ledbetter, known as Leadbelly, was such a great country blues singer that a warden pardoned him for the crime of murder and released him from jail. Robert Johnson, a legendary player from Texas, led such a mysterious life that some believed he had sold his soul to the devil in exchange for his musical ability. He was murdered in his twenties, poisoned by a man who believed Johnson was flirting with the man's wife.

Not all blues singers lived short, unhappy lives. Memphis Slim, for one, first migrated to Chicago, then went to live the life of a sophisticate in Paris in the 1960s. He wrote enduring songs such as "Every Day."

In the 1920s, many southern African-Americans began moving North to cities such as Chicago, Kansas City, and New York. Among them were gospel and blues singers, both men and women. People left behind poverty and total segregation for freer living conditions in the

Son House was one of the great guitar-playing blues singers who put secular lyrics to gospel music.

Swingers and Crooners

North. Many sought factory jobs and housework as cleaners, cooks, and baby nurses. They found ways to start businesses, such as beauty parlors, restaurants, rooming houses, and tailor shops. Occasionally a small business developed into a big one. Some people entered professions, too.

They still faced prejudice and hardship. But they worked in buildings instead of on farms, and they earned more money in the North. Their lifestyles became faster paced. Those with little education sometimes tried to get more, even if it was just vocational training. They became more sophisticated in their manners, clothing styles, and understanding of the world.

In the North, blues singers sang stories about their new circumstances. Rich or poor, people found themselves all alone in a crowd of strangers at times. Far from relatives and friends in familiar southern neighborhoods, they felt lonely and isolated, as immigrants often do. Down home, people had known each other. In a big, cold, impersonal city, relationships between strangers were filled with surprises, sometimes unpleasant ones. Even the weather gave people the blues.

The invention of the carbon microphone in 1920 had a profound effect on all musicians. In clubs and theaters, because of the microphone, audiences could hear singers clearly. It picked up every sound. Bad singers had their careers ruined; others who had small but wonderful voices or styles became stars. Recordings by blues singers were produced in greater numbers and sold to customers around the country.

One recording gave a big boost to blues singers in New York City in 1920 or 1921. Singer Mamie Smith recorded a song called "Crazy Blues." The record was first sold in little stores and from the backs of trucks in Harlem. People fell in love with the song, and soon the record couldn't be produced fast enough to satisfy the demand.

Record company owners, who had been selling songs by white singers in shops catering to white customers, suddenly realized they could do big business with the blues for African-Americans. So companies started divisions that produced music called "race records." White people around the country heard these recordings, too, of course. White entertainers learned from the best blues singers.

About two hundred African-American women singers recorded the blues in the 1920s. One of the best known was Gertrude "Ma" Rainey, a Southerner, who traveled from town to town to perform. She took along a young protégé named Bessie Smith, a tall, plump, stunning-looking woman. Bessie had such a rich, powerful voice that she didn't need a microphone to make herself heard in the top balconies of theaters. She became even more famous than Ma Rainey. Her records sold incredibly well, and she filled every seat with fans in theaters in Chicago and every other city where she performed.

One of Bessie's admirers, Mildred Bailey, was a white woman who lived in the state of Washington. Mildred influenced many other white singers, including Bing Crosby, who, like Nat Cole, became a legendary jazz-influenced singer.

Bessie Smith often traveled around the country in her own train car. That way she could avoid the idiocy and insult of segregation, which prevented her from eating in a dining car and sleeping in a bed. In her own car, she took along all the food, gowns, equipment, and helpers she needed.

In New York, she became the darling of wealthy socialites, who brought her to sing in their homes for private parties. She made the blues and the blues culture even better known. Her songs, with their special rhythms and blue notes—the flatted, mournful sounding notes that African-American singers improvised when they glided between the written notes—enchanted all audiences.

The blues, which was the foundation of jazz singing, remained popular until the early 1930s. One of the most important record producers who loved the blues was John Hammond, a member of the wealthy Vanderbilt family. He wrote a column for a British jazz magazine, *Melody Maker*, and he recorded Bessie Smith for Columbia Records. He had fallen in love with Bessie's voice the moment he heard it, and his recordings of her became an important part of the country's musical and cultural history. By the 1930s, though, Bessie was down on her luck, singing for a little bit of money in a Philadelphia club. She had become a victim of her own heavy drinking and other personal problems. Furthermore, new developments in music were leaving her behind.

Every ten years or so, the fashion in popular music changes in America. People who had loved the blues during World War I changed their minds during the Depression years beginning in 1929. The blues was primarily a mournful, simple, folk music. People wanted to cheer up during the 1930s and escape from the problems of the country's financial calamity. So a different style of music, which had been developing in the 1920s, caught the public fancy.

The new style used some elements of the blues and was actually an extension of the blues. But it was more upbeat and modern, played at quicker tempos. The songs were often about idealized romance. The new style could use a blues form, but also used 32-bar tunes—classic American pop songs, some borrowed from American musical theater headquartered in New York City. All of the material was played in a swinging style. In its earliest days, as it developed, it was often called ragtime. By the 1920s and 1930s, it became known as jazz and swing.

The person usually credited with inventing jazz and helping to popularize swing was a trumpeter and singer born in New Orleans, Louisiana—Louis Armstrong. For his genius as a jazz inventor, for his role as a leader in so much of the development of jazz music, Louis Armstrong became known to other instrumentalists and singers as "Pops."

Chapter Two The Legacy of Louis Armstrong

Part One: A Child of New Orleans

New Orleans is a beautiful, warm port city with a Caribbean ambiance at the mouth of the muddy, churning Mississippi River. The Spanish ruled it at the end of the eighteenth century. Emperor Napoléon Bonaparte, France's great military leader, took it over for France and then sold it to the United States in 1803 in a deal called the Louisiana Purchase. Boats with all sorts of goods and a great number of people with different backgrounds were always coming and going. They made New Orleans an exotic and important port.

Different cultures and races blended there—whites from many countries, descendants of former African slaves, American Indians, and French-speaking Cajuns who had migrated from Canada to the nearby swampy bayou country in Louisiana. From these diverse groups arose a

In the port of New Orleans, the singing styles of many ethnic groups and nationalities mingled, and the city was filled with music.

new class of people called Creoles. People of color mingled more freely with whites in nineteenth-century New Orleans than they did in the rest of the South. Wealthy white fathers with talented Creole children often sent the children to Paris to study music.

But in the 1890s, segregation became the law. Creoles of mixed race were demoted in status. By law, life became meaner for African-Americans or anyone with even a small percentage of African heritage.

However, the multicultural citizens of New Orleans didn't care to end their freewheeling lifestyle. The sultry, humid weather, the artistic, elaborate French architecture with wrought-iron lattice work, and the Mississippi River added to the sensual, dreamy, even mysterious atmosphere. New Orleans had always had a dual personality. The majority of people were Catholics, with strict ideas about proper behavior. But everyone still wanted to have a good time.

Many people headed for Storyville, a part of town divided into white and African-American sections and filled with honky-tonks, bars, clubs, and brothels. Some places were well known as "black and tans," where African-Americans and whites socialized, often for illicit entertainment. Police were supposed to enforce segregation, but in fact they were paid to look the other way. Everybody wanted to hear music in these places.

Holidays that were celebrated for a day in other cities lasted a week in New Orleans. People liked to join private clubs that sponsored parties. Every weekend, club members staged picnics by the Mississippi River or Lake Pontchartrain, which bounded the city. People brought plenty to eat and drink, threw sawdust on the ground, and danced all night. They hired little bands to provide the music. Musicians were often paid with hot dogs and drinks. After work on Fridays, everybody went out "good-timing" some place in town, and they didn't go back to work until "Blue Monday" ended.[1]

African-American musicians traveled around town in trucks, singing and playing in different neighborhoods. They passed a hat to collect tips as payment. Talented children formed sidewalk quartets and sang and danced for people in the streets. Even funerals in New Orleans were jubilant celebrations.

When someone died, especially a man whom other people liked or respected, he was treated to a genuine New Orleans funeral. He was placed in a coffin on a carriage drawn by white horses. His fellow club members dressed up in their uniforms and hired a band to march with them. (Most men belonged to clubs in those days.) The band played a sad, slow dirge as it followed the mourners and the coffin to the cemetery. Popular songs for funerals were "Jesus, Lover of My Soul" and "Nearer My God to Thee." After the dead person was buried, the mourners headed back to town.

On the way back into town, the band speeded up the tempo of the music and played joyful songs in a two-beat rhythm. People clapped their hands to that steady, syncopated beat. "When the Saints Go Marching In" was a favorite hymn. The New Orleans style made it a happy music to help the mourners get over their sorrow.

The funeral tradition, which dates back to the nineteenth century, still exists today. Not only does a band play, but strangers who never knew the dead person join in. They dance and play instruments, too, and are called the "Second Line." The whole funeral procession has come to be known as the Second Line.

Budding young musicians have always regarded New Orleans as an ideal place to grow up. It was in this music-oriented culture of New Orleans that a little boy named Louis Armstrong was born to a very poor African-American family in 1901—"from the bottom of the well, one step from hell."[2] Every day he heard gospel hymns in the churches, Second Line funeral bands, blues in the honky-tonks near his home, Cajun music played with accordions, violins, and percussion, African-derived drumming rituals, the two-beat syncopated music used in carnivals that developed from a blend of African traditions and European harmonies, music from minstrel shows and vaudeville theaters, the

20

music of classically-trained Creole and white musicians, the haunting Spanish-influenced melodies brought to town by visitors from Caribbean countries, and bands at lakeside parties on weekends. Before he was ten, Louis began singing the soprano part with a sidewalk quartet of little boys.

He was working with his quartet downtown one New Year's Eve when everybody, including Louis, was in high spirits. He heard a boy across the street fire a pistol into the air. Though it was illegal, people in New Orleans would do this on holidays. Louis had borrowed a pistol belonging to one of his mother's boyfriends and fired it to show off to his friends and join in the noisy celebration.

Suddenly a white policeman grabbed him. Louis begged not to be arrested, but the policeman locked him up in a jail cell. At dawn, a judge decided Louis was a wayward boy and sentenced him for an indefinite period to the Colored Waifs School for Boys on the edge of town. For the first three days, he missed his family so much that he didn't eat.

He tried to adjust to the school and decided to join the school band. He started on the tambourine and drums, but eventually the music teacher let him try a cornet. Louis practiced constantly and became so good that he was appointed leader of the band. That was an important step for him. The school helped to support itself with the earnings of its student band, which traveled on a truck and entertained in different neighborhoods in New Orleans. When the band went to Storyville, Louis's mother and all her neighbors came out to hear him play. He was wearing a brown- and cream-colored uniform that he loved. He felt proud that his neighbors in the tough Storyville section of town, poor as they were (and some of them underworld hustlers), donated big tips to the band.

Louis impressed older musicians who heard him playing cornet. Some of them would become internationally known; many traveled up the Mississippi River to play in St. Louis, Chicago, and New York clubs. They would also make recordings right in New Orleans, and their music was circulated around the world. One important cornetist in New Orleans, Joe "King" Oliver, took an interest in Louis and advised him about playing.

When Louis got out of the Colored Waifs home, he went home to his mother, Mayann, whom he loved. She was a friendly woman who told Louis never to be a snob. She praised him and taught him little tricks about staying healthy. She especially wanted him to take a physic regularly. When he was a little older, they sometimes went to clubs together.

King Oliver and other musicians kept encouraging him. They went to hear him singing and playing by the curbsides, and they hired him to play on trucks, at picnics, in honky-tonks, and in funerals. Oliver gave Louis a new cornet to replace the banged-up instrument he had bought in a pawn shop. And Oliver and his wife invited Louis to dinner, where they served him his favorite food, red beans and rice, a popular "soul food" in New Orleans.

King Oliver went up the Mississippi River to St. Louis on a boat, and from there traveled by train all the way to Chicago, where he formed his own band. For a while, Louis took Oliver's place in the best band in New Orleans, which was led by trombonist Edward "Kid" Ory. Louis switched to trumpet, and he kept developing his unique style based on the mixture of musical styles he had heard in New Orleans. By embellishing everything he heard in New Orleans, and making his blend swing with Dixieland's characteristic two-beat rhythm, he was creating modern jazz.

He sang in exactly the same style with which he played his horn. Every singer and instrumentalist who came along after him would look up to him as the originator and the master. Danny Barker, a fine New Orleans guitar and banjo player, eight years younger than Louis, knew all about Louis's musical influences and education. Louis had heard scat singing, songs without words, "monkey-shine singing," as Danny said it was called. He believed it came from the Cajuns in the bayous.

Louis also paid special attention in the early 1920s to recordings by the early blues and popular singers, such as Bessie Smith, who was called "Empress of the Blues," and a slender pop singer, Ethel Waters, nicknamed "Sweet Mama Stringbean." Bessie was already touring the country and working in New York City clubs in the 1920s. Ethel had a pretty soprano; her high notes sounded like the chimes of a silver spoon tapping a crystal glass. Armstrong heard many other singers, too, when they played at the Lyric Theater in New Orleans or simply entertained in the streets and the joints.

Armstrong also liked the way the ragtime piano players treated music, playing all the notes in a chord. He started playing them, too, instead of just the one note that the trumpeter was supposed to play. He also played notes that the chords suggested to him—notes that fit in well with the written chords. Musicians called the technique "blowing on the changes." (Chords were referred to as "changes" because the notes of a chord could be changed.) By blowing on the changes, Armstrong was improvising. That is part of the way that he created modern jazz. He bent the notes, gliding from one to another, for a deeper, more plaintive, emotionally stirring sound. Just as he played two notes or as many as eight notes for the one written note in a song, he also sang those notes. In this way, Louis was also the founder of modern jazz singing.

His voice changed from soprano to baritone. Then it became a little gruff. Eventually it became very rough. People in New Orleans and everywhere else were enchanted by his style, his creativity, his freshness, and his brash sound. "So many people died of trying to imitate Louis, sticking their heads out of windows in a blizzard," Danny Barker explained in a humorous way about the effect Armstrong had on other singers. "They died of choking, trying to get that raspy voice like Satchmo's. Before him, singers were known as coloraturas, tenors, lyric sopranos, or basso profundos [in classical music]. There were blues, opera, gospel, folk and pop singers. But Armstrong said: A cat sings from his soul, with feeling. It didn't matter about his voice. The style was how he sang, in his phrasing. Most trumpet players were playing staccato.

Swingers and Crooners

Louis Armstrong began playing legato and soaring on the notes with long phrases. He sang the same way. To see him in person was exhilarating. He scooped up every thing he had ever heard in Storyville and everyplace else and put it together."

In 1922, King Oliver, who had started his own band in Chicago, invited Louis to join the group. By then Louis was twenty-one years old. (He would always claim that he had been born on July 4, 1900, but he was actually born in 1901; he wanted to get a draft card and present himself as a little more mature than he was, especially when he searched for jobs.[3]) King Oliver had actually invited Armstrong before 1922, but Louis had hesitated. He had been happy working in New Orleans and on the riverboats that traveled on the Mississippi River up to St. Louis and back. And he had married a slightly older woman named Daisy. A prostitute who worked in honky-tonks, she sometimes snatched purses and fought with customers in the bars. But Armstrong fell in love with her. In those days, he mingled with hustlers and assorted tough characters in Storyville. But he kept himself out of a life of criminal activities, because he loved his horn. He knew his love for music was his saving grace.

By 1922, however, he and Daisy were fighting too much. He felt he had to get away from her. He told his mother he was going to join King Oliver in Chicago. Mayann escorted him to the boat and gave him a fish sandwich to begin his journey.

Farther up the country, he switched to a train. He was late arriving in Chicago. King Oliver had gone to the station to meet him. When Louis didn't show up, Oliver had to hurry to the club where he was leading his band. Louis made his way there alone. Standing outside, he felt intimidated by the sight of Chicago's big buildings, the fast pace of the street traffic, and the sound of the band swinging inside. He nearly turned around to catch a train back to New Orleans. But he decided to step inside the club for a minute. King Oliver was delighted to see him. Louis felt safe, and he stayed in Chicago.

Part Two: Man of the World

It was a revolutionary time for musicians and singers, with the invention of the microphone and mass-produced recordings. Armstrong made records with blues singers and with King Oliver's band. He met a woman named Lil Hardin, a pianist, who encouraged and advised him about how to run his own groups, which he called Hot Five and Hot Seven bands. Louis and Lil got married, and she played in his groups. As his records circulated through the country, musicians got a chance to hear his thrilling style and tone on trumpet. A white singer named Al Jolson, an important star in the 1920s and 1930s, heard Armstrong's records. And Bing Crosby, who would become one of the country's best and most popular singers, revered Jolson's style. So indirectly, Bing felt Louis's influence even before he heard Armstrong in person in Chicago in the 1920s. Bing knew a hip, natural sound when he heard it. He would start to make movies with Armstrong in the 1930s.

Early in his career, Louis was most in demand for his trumpet playing. Lil encouraged him to go to work in New York, where he made a hit playing with a highly respected African-American band led by Fletcher Henderson. Visiting Chicago briefly, Henderson had heard Louis and invited him to add his brilliance to the band. Louis recorded with Henderson, made a big impression on New York musicians, and returned to Chicago to work in the orchestra pit at the Vendome Theater for bandleader Erskine Hawkins. Crowds flocked there to hear Armstrong play countless high Cs at every performance. Sometimes he played so hard that his top lip bled by the end of the night.

In 1928, Armstrong performed an extraordinary vocal and instrumental recording of a song called "West End Blues." The musingly scatted and hummed vocal version had a dreamy beauty. It sounded like a reverie. And it was a perfect jazz song because of Armstrong's spontaneity and flirtatious, carefree spirit. It became a jazz classic. Some critics have called it the first genuine, thoroughly modern jazz song. The song fits the definition of jazz coined by a genius who came on the scene later—alto saxophonist Charlie "Bird" Parker, who called jazz "a happiness blues."

Few musicians have ever agreed upon an exact definition of jazz, but most say it must contain improvisation, and it must swing or imply dance rhythms derived from the old rhythmic device of syncopation. Syncopation is the rhythm achieved by stressing the weak beat in a measure of music. Louis Armstrong's style made him sound as if he wrote his swinging songs on the spur of the moment. His naturalness became a guide and a goal for every jazz singer and musician.

Ray Charles and Billie Holiday were two budding stars who fell under Armstrong's spell when they heard how he phrased and embellished songs on his early recordings. They loved the way he communicated feeling. Trumpeter and singer Louis Prima would become well-known for singing in a scratchy voice like Satchmo's. Musicians revered Armstrong's style so much that they started calling him "Pops." (He acquired several nicknames. The most popular was "Satchelmouth" for his wide, big mouth; a British critic shortened it to "Satchmo.")

In 1929, returning to New York, Armstrong was asked to sing and play a song called "Ain't Misbehavin' " by composer, pianist, organist, and singer Fats Waller, a star in his own right. Waller and Armstrong had become close friends during Armstrong's first visit to Harlem. "Ain't Misbehavin' " was a song in an African-American show called *Hot Chocolates*, which opened on Broadway on July 23, 1929. Armstrong sang between the acts. His style quickly earned him rave reviews from critics and a special credit line in the program. A new star was born on Broadway.

By 1932, he was so popular that he went to London, England, and played at the Palladium Theater. In a command performance for the king and queen, he called out to them from the stage, addressing them as "Kingsie" and "Queensie." They loved it. He was invited to dine with the royal family, and they enjoyed his company.

He performed around the world for the rest of his life. In 1947, when his big band became too costly to support, he played with a small group at Town Hall in New York. The results were so exciting and critically acclaimed that he decided to work with a small group all the time. He called it the All Stars, and he traveled with it from then on.

He had the physical stamina to travel for months on end in a bus that was too hot in summer and too cold in winter. He bumped along over rocky roads. He slept in his seat. Many musicians he hired came and went because they couldn't stand the hardships. But Armstrong never quit. His voice became raspier, because of all the vibrant high Cs and upper-register straining that he had done with his horn. The raspier his singing voice became, the more popular he was.

He played in many movies. In time, he began to get better parts. His early roles had often been silly, even racially demeaning. In one role, he wore an animal skin. But his music always sounded wonderful no matter what role he played. He had a small acting part that he handled with aplomb in *Paris Blues* with Paul Newman. Even as an actor, Satchmo was a natural.

One of Louis's best movies was *High Society*, made with Grace Kelly, Bing Crosby, Frank Sinatra, and Celeste Holm. The movie opened with Armstrong traveling on a bus into Newport, Rhode Island, where he was going to play for a society wedding. He sang his great hit, "High Society," dragging out the words "High—high—high—high—high—So -Ci -Uh -Teeeeeee." His music was sparkling and invigorating; without it, the movie would actually have been boring. He even made the bridal march swing at the end of the story and then launched into "High Society" again, with special lyrics in honor of hero Bing Crosby and heroine Grace Kelly. The song made the movie end with the proper, upbeat, jubilant feeling.

Louis became a goodwill ambassador for the United States government despite his distress at prejudice against African-Americans and at the violence that erupted from the country's early attempts to desegre-

This photo shows "Pops" Armstrong, as he was called, in the 1961 movie Paris Blues, *in which he had a fine cameo acting role.*

gate schools and public facilities. He voiced his protests through the news media. J. Edgar Hoover, the powerful head of the Federal Bureau of Investigation, began to keep a file on Armstrong.

But Satchmo kept traveling for the government. His trumpet playing and his singing were able to reach across footlights, country borders, and political ideologies. He personally bridged the gap between the Western world's democratic societies and the dictatorships of Eastern Europe. Politicians and statesmen failed to reach understandings, but Satchmo kept the lines of communication between people open.

Armstrong recorded so many songs that he could barely recall many of them. One of the most inconsequential of them, he thought at first, was the show tune "Hello, Dolly." Armstrong was appearing with his All Stars in a Chicago club in 1963 when an executive from Kapp Records in New York telephoned and asked him to come to New York and record some songs. Once there, Armstrong was handed the sheet music to "Hello, Dolly." He looked at it and didn't like it. "You mean you brought us all the way from Chicago to play this?" he said. The All Stars recorded it and went back on tour. Every place they went, Louis was asked to sing "Hello, Dolly." He didn't know what people were talking about. One night in Nebraska, he turned to his bassist Arvel Shaw and said, "What's that?" Arvel said, "Don't you remember?" But Louis didn't. He had to send to New York for the sheet music, so he could learn the song again. It became one of his biggest hits.

Louis also had a hit with the Kurt Weill song "Mack the Knife," about a denizen of the underworld, from the Viennese composer's *Three-penny Opera*. Armstrong's great ease, authority, and humorous approach to that song may have come in part from his memories of the rough characters who had been his companions in Storyville.

He was accused of selling out to commercialism because he sang so many popular songs. Of his singing, he said, "I sang some in Chicago, but it didn't get big until New York when the arrangers like Gordon Jenkins [in the 1950s] made up the arrangements with me singing that chorus. I just went along with whatever they brought for me. Everybody liked the singing and I never was trying to prove anything. Just wanted to give a good show."[4]

He was best known among jazz fans for singing his standard, Southern-flavored jazz songs, such as "Muskrat Ramble," "I'll Be Glad When You're Dead, You Rascal, You," "Dinah," "When It's Sleepy Time Down South," and the classic, "What Did I Do To Be So Black and Blue?" His fans had their favorite old Dixieland songs by Armstrong. He often introduced a song as "one of the good old good ones." He could give an audience goose pimples with his version of "St. James Infirmary," a song about saying farewell to his sweetheart, his "baby," lying cold and dead in a morgue. He ended with instructions about the fine clothes and jewelry he wanted to wear for his own burial. In Armstrong's version, the song mixed the sad and joyful feeling of the Second Line.

For many years, he hired a woman, Velma Middleton, to sing with the All Stars. He was criticized, because Velma, an obese woman, had a rough voice and did acrobatic splits on stage. But some of the funnier onstage vignettes in jazz singing happened because of the chemistry between Armstrong and Velma, his professional soul sister.

From the first bars of a song such as "That's My Desire," about a romantic rendezvous, Velma used Armstrong's exact phrasing. She had absorbed his style completely to enhance his performance. When he chimed in, gravel-voiced: "Mmmmmmm, that's my desire," she gave the response, "Mine, too." In the song Armstrong talked about mingling his lips with Velma's, but Armstrong called them "chops." He changed other words, too. Instead of simply saying that it was time to go, as the lyrics were written, Armstrong first said "doggone," then the drummer's sticks produced the sound of horses' hooves. And Louis often simply scatted words, with great effect. "Babababababababa" he sang in reply to Velma's line saying she knew he had found a new girlfriend. Armstrong respected the subtle wit that had always been an important element in jazz and helped make the music a form of social commentary.

The Legacy of Louis Armstrong

After Velma died of a stroke during a tour in Africa, Armstrong mourned her death deeply. He never filled her position again to his liking. Even so, he and another jazz singing superstar, Ella Fitzgerald, became wildly famous for duets together, she with her ecstatic soprano, he with a voice described by one critic as "the mating call of a piece of sandpaper."[5]

In his sixties, Armstrong's heart began to fail. He kept going from hospital beds to his house in Corona, Queens, New York, where his last wife, Lucille, took care of him, to his bus on the road. Lucille had insisted that they buy a house and stop living in hotels. But his life was lived primarily as a traveling musician—a real troubadour.

Early in 1971, quite sick, he played at the elegant Waldorf-Astoria Hotel in New York City. Then he appeared as a guest on several television shows. In February, at his home in Corona, he recorded the narrative poem, "'Twas the Night Before Christmas," improvising his own jazzy slang expressions for some of the written words. The record is still played on radio stations during the Christmas season. He had a heart attack a few weeks later. Out of the hospital by May, feeling better—but bored—he decided to go back to work in July. He called the All Stars to come to a rehearsal. A few hours before they were scheduled to arrive, he died in his sleep.

Danny Barker convinced the city of New Orleans to erect a statue of Armstrong on the site of what had once been a slave market—the old Congo Square. Now it's a beautiful park with duck ponds. An entrance gate bears Armstrong's name. Danny Barker gave a speech at the unveiling. He told people that serious students should listen to Armstrong's natural speech style, and his immense humor, and compare his style with the way popular music sounded before him. Before Armstrong, horn players had tried to sound like singers. Armstrong changed the emphasis. The goal of singers became to sound like horns with the fluidity, swing, and tone of Armstrong's style. Danny Barker reminded people at the unveiling how great Armstrong's contribution to American popular music and jazz had been.

Swingers and Crooners

Even during the height of the popularity of the Beatles in the 1960s, Armstrong's "Hello Dolly" went to the top of the charts. And a NASA Voyager spacecraft sent into orbit in the 1970s carried a mixture of examples of American culture; it included twenty-seven different pieces of music, and the one jazz tune was "Melancholy Blues," performed by Armstrong. The 1987 movie *Good Morning, Vietnam* used Armstrong's recording, "What a Wonderful World," for the soundtrack. The whimsical, dreamy song, with Armstrong's scratchy but musing voice, became a major hit.

A much younger jazz singer, Dave Frishberg, explained Armstrong's magic: "He really brings life to the music."

Chapter Three **Early Singing Stars**

The singers who incorporated the gregarious Armstrong's ideas into their own styles came from every possible type of background. Al Jolson was born in Russia; his father, a Jewish cantor, wanted him to sing religious music. But Jolson loved musical theater, minstrel shows, vaudeville, and the African-American music he heard in Baltimore, Maryland, where he grew up. Becoming one of the most popular singers in the history of the country, he starred in the first "talkie" movie, *The Jazz Singer*. Bing Crosby, born in 1904, loved the Irish singers he heard as a child in Tacoma and Spokane, Washington. Bing thought Jolson's singing was so irresistible that he dropped out of law school to try a career in popular music.

Sophie Tucker, a blues singer and vaudeville comedian who was born while her parents were moving between Poland and Russia, was influenced by Bessie Smith. Mildred Bailey's father was Irish, and her mother, who was part Coeur d'Alene Indian, could play classical music and ragtime on the piano. Nobody knew where Mildred's mother had heard ragtime in those pre-radio days. Born Mildred Rinker in 1907 (she took the name Bailey from her first marriage), Mildred grew up near Spokane, Washington, too. As luck would have it, her brother, Al Rinker, also a singer, and Bing Crosby were boyhood friends.

Mildred was a very short, heavy woman, and she was difficult and moody. Her second husband, bandleader Red Norvo, said she argued with staffers in recording studios because they simply weren't accustomed to a woman setting tempos in those days. Mildred fought to put across her musical ideas. That was one reason she acquired the reputation of being difficult. But she was always fighting, even with her husband. (They eventually divorced.) She felt that her size kept her from becoming a better-known star. Even so, the public loved her girlishly clear, warm voice. When she developed diabetes, she kept eating the wrong foods. She died in 1951, at age forty-four. She particularly influenced white women singers, including pretty, blonde Lee Wiley, who was also part Indian.

Fats Waller, a composer, singer, and musician in the musical comedy tradition, was born and brought up in New York City. He established a bright career in Harlem and on recordings at the same time Armstrong was starting out in Chicago. When Armstrong went to New York in 1924, he and Waller became friends, and Waller went back to Chicago with Armstrong in 1925.

Waller, the leading stride piano player in Harlem in the 1920s, 1930s, and 1940s, appeared in movies and toured the country. His style is immortalized in such movies as *Stormy Weather*, in which he sang his own composition, "Ain't Misbehavin'." In a room filled with pretty girls, he sang to each one that he was saving his love for her. He accompanied many blues singers on records. And he wrote wonderful songs that became American pop and jazz standard classics. Unfortunately his

34

health was weakened by a drinking problem, and he died young from pneumonia. Many years later, his songs and the story of his life became a hit on Broadway in a show called *Ain't Misbehavin'*.

Ethel Waters had been acclaimed as a blues and pop singer before she ever heard a recording by Armstrong. But she said that she learned some musical phrases—musicians call them "licks" or "riffs"—from Louis.

All of these singers had an enormous impact on other singers. Among the singers who had the longest-lasting influence were Bing Crosby and Ethel Waters.

Bing Crosby

Paul Whiteman led one of the most popular swing-era dance bands beginning in the 1920s. In 1929, traveling through Los Angeles, he heard Bing Crosby and Al Rinker singing together in a vaudeville show at a theater. Bing and Al had packed all their belongings into Al's old car and had driven from the state of Washington to try their luck in Los Angeles, where they lived with Al's sister, Mildred. Whiteman hired the delightful duo—Bing with his laid-back, smooth baritone, and Rinker with his jazzy cadences.

Whiteman added another singer, Harry Barris, to create a trio known as the Rhythm Boys. Audiences loved them. When Whiteman's band played in Chicago, Bing went to hear Louis Armstrong play trumpet and sing in a South Side club. That's when Bing fell in love with Satchmo's swinging, natural style.

Whiteman's band returned to Los Angeles, where Al Rinker introduced Whiteman to his sister Mildred, who was working in a little club in town. Whiteman was so charmed by her pure, swinging style when she sang "Sleepy Time Gal" that he hired her on the spot. For her debut on his radio show, she sang "Moaning Low." She was earning $75 a week then, but within a year he had raised her salary to $1,250 a week—she was that important to the band's success. She became famous for singing "Rockin' Chair." Mildred may have been the first "girl singer" to sing with any big band.

The Rhythm Boys, also boosted by their days with Whiteman, went out on their own. When they played the Cocoanut Grove in Los Angeles, Bing emerged as the romantic star of the group. Harry Barris was angry about it. But Bing decided to go on alone. In the 1930s, he was headlining at the Paramount Theatre in New York, singing for five shows a day.

Late each night, he went to Harlem clubs to listen for ideas and put finishing touches on his work. Harlem nearly put the finishing touches on Crosby in another way, because Bing liked to drink whiskey so much. He was nicknamed "Binge," and his drinking nearly ruined his career, but he later overcame it.

Bing Crosby's career as a singer continued for almost fifty years. He became famous for his acting, too, beginning with the movie *The Big Broadcast of 1932*. In 1933, Chesterfield cigarettes gave him a radio contract. After that, he was always on radio and then television. Starting in 1940, he teamed up with comedian Bob Hope and actress Dorothy Lamour for their very successful series of road films—*Road To Singapore, Road to Rio*, and many others. Bing won an Academy Award for *Going My Way*, in which he played a priest; he was nominated for awards for its sequel, *The Bells of St. Mary's*, and for his role as an alcoholic actor in *The Country Girl*.

Bing Crosby had many imitators. Perry Como was one of the best. The legendary Fred Astaire, an eccentric, balletic-athletic tap dancer, admired Crosby's singing style. For movies, Astaire was asked to sing some of the great standard songs when they were newly written by Cole Porter, Irving Berlin, George and Ira Gershwin, and Johnny Mercer. Astaire simply let himself be guided by his friend Bing's natural approach to singing, as well as by his own dancer's feeling for rhythm. Singing about raindrops, Astaire slowed the tempo and delivered the words in a way that made them sound like the drip of individual drops

Bing Crosby, shown here singing with Irving Aaronson and his orchestra in Los Angeles in 1934, rose from the ranks of the big-band singers to become one of the country's greatest early jazz stars. His career ran the gamut of theaters, radio, television, and movies.

on a windowsill. He could make lyrics seem lighter than air, just as his dancer's body seemed to be in his complicated choreographed steps.

But nobody was as popular as Bing, who had one of the most natural sounding styles, with easy swing and offhand phrasing. A great deal of thought went into his delivery of lyrics. In one of his movies, he gave a lesson to a budding singer, telling her to stop moving so much and to sing the words with respect for their meaning. His control made the acrobatic things he did with his voice sound simple and conversational. He had a warm, deep baritone, which never seemed to change. It even became monotonous because he sang and recorded so much. But his mellow, sensuous tone helped him glide and swing through the decades as a superstar.

Like Louis Armstrong, Bing never lost his popular appeal because his sound had the feeling of home. His was a smooth and reassuring sound. Bing could sing about love and passion, God, holidays, and passing seasons with glib control, with his confident swing based lightly upon the gregariousness of Louis and the two-beat rhythm of Dixieland.

Ethel Waters

By the 1920s, Harlem had become a thriving community for African-Americans. Though it was a poor community, it attracted some of the most talented African-American writers, painters, and especially entertainers. Downtown theaters hired the cream of the white entertainment world, while Harlem's clubs and theaters featured the African-Americans, sometimes for audiences of mixed races, but often for whites only. Harlem's Cotton Club, a legendary nightclub with a chorus line of beautiful women, starred Duke Ellington and his orchestra. When Ellington toured, Cab Calloway took over. Run by gangsters, the Cotton

Club catered only to white audiences. They went uptown in furs and limousines for the shows.

By 1925, Ethel Waters's recording of a song called "Dinah" brought her national attention. When she toured, a critic for a Chicago newspaper wrote, "A new star is discovered on State Street. Ethel Waters is the greatest artist of her race and generation."

Little is known about her earliest musical influences. She was born in 1897—or perhaps even a few years before that—in Chester, Pennsylvania, near Philadelphia. She was the illegitimate child of a twelve-year-old girl, Louisa Anderson, who had been raped by a man named John Wesley Waters. When she became famous, Ethel wrote her autobiography, *His Eye Is on the Sparrow*, taking the title from a sublime gospel hymn. But the details of her early life were nightmarish. Her mother was cold to her, and her grandmother, who worked as a maid, took care of her, bringing her along to jobs and singing to her.

Since Ethel's grandmother was Catholic, Ethel didn't go to Protestant churches to hear gospel singers. She heard vaudeville entertainers and enough blues singers to borrow their lines, such as "The nearer the bone, the sweeter the meat." She admired Bessie Smith and Mamie Smith, though in her autobiography Ethel wrote that she had her own low, sweet style instead of Bessie's "loud approach." She was enchanted by "St. Louis Blues," which she first heard sung by a female impersonator.

Working as a maid in a hotel, she watched show people come and go. She practiced singing in front of mirrors and mustered up the nerve to enter an amateur contest. Her victory there excited two of her friends. They said they would manage her career, and they booked her into a Baltimore club for twenty-five dollars a week. But they gave her only nine dollars of it. She left them in the dust and went on the African-American vaudeville circuit called the Theatre Owners Booking Association, nicknamed TOBA. (African-American entertainers said that TOBA stood for Tough on Black Asses.)

Ethel Waters had a nationwide hit with "Dinah" in 1925. She was hailed as one of "the greatest artists of her race and generation" by a Chicago newspaper critic.

When she reached Harlem, she went to work in Edmond Johnson's Cellar, where audiences loved to hear her sing sexy blues songs filled with subtle jokes, such as "My Handy Man Ain't Handy No More." She didn't like that type of song, but she sang what her audiences shouted for. And she liked Harlem and stayed in Johnson's Cellar for a long time. Eventually, she became known for singing sophisticated, popular songs of the day, such as "Supper Time," a lament by a wife whose husband wouldn't be coming home for supper anymore because he had been lynched, and "Stormy Weather," about a woman who was unhappy because her man had left her. The great songwriter Irving Berlin wrote "Supper Time" especially for her. She often had tears in her eyes when she sang "Stormy Weather," because it reminded her of the troubles in her marriage. When she stopped crying during that song, her husband told a friend that he knew the marriage was ending.

Ethel could sing the Queen's English, though it's doubtful she could read it. And she couldn't read music. She learned songs by hearing them a few times. But she could hit high notes that sounded like a silver spoon ringing on a crystal glass, at the beat of her choice. Her soprano could drop quickly to a rich contralto. Not only did she have a beautiful voice, but she phrased the words in such an arresting way, with great feeling, that her songs held audiences rapt. Sophie Tucker went to hear Ethel. With her loud, shouting style, Sophie obviously was influenced by Bessie Smith, but she became so impressed by Ethel that she asked for lessons, or at least for technical advice.

Ethel recorded the blues with several fine swing-era bands, including Fletcher Henderson's. A pianist named Lou Henley helped her learn new pop tunes. Soon she went to replace the best-known popular singer of the day, Florence Mills, at the Plantation Club on 50th Street and Broadway in New York. She was afraid to travel to Paris at the time, so she turned down an invitation to sing there. A young dancer named Josephine Baker went instead and became a legendary dancer and singer in Europe. Josephine had worked in a chorus behind Ethel and learned everything about singing from her; Baker copied Ethel's rolled "r".

Swingers and Crooners

Ethel starred in *Lew Leslie's Blackbirds* in 1930, *Rhapsodies in Black* in 1931, and *As Thousands Cheer* in 1932. She also continued singing in clubs. Her salary rose from about $175 in the 1920s to $1,250 a week and more in the 1930s. She recorded for Columbia and Decca. Captured on film when she was young, she was effervescent, pretty, and bright-eyed, and so slim that she was nicknamed "Sweet Mama Stringbean."

Aspiring singers went to her shows and tried to learn from her style. They said she was an expert at delineating her stories. That is, she painted scenes and conjured up visual images for audiences. A singer named Thelma Carpenter discovered that Ethel Waters had no particular role models. She had simply created an original style, fusing musical theater techniques and blues feeling.

Ethel Waters became very heavy as she grew older. By the time she acted in a movie called *Cabin in the Sky*, with an all-African-American cast, she felt jealous of her younger co-star Lena Horne, one of the great beauties of the century. Waters had other problems as well. She earned a great deal of money, but she lacked the education to deal with it; she didn't take care of her tax obligations or put her money in banks. She gave big sums away to friends, to boyfriends, and to Eddie Matthews, a gambler and a hustler. (He was probably her only legal husband, though she was rumored to have married three or four times.) Eventually she had serious tax problems with the Internal Revenue Service.

But her talent endured. She was so eloquent that, when she was given the chance to act, she became better known as an actress than a singer by the 1950s. She became a star on Broadway in *The Member of the Wedding*, in which her character befriends and saves the life of a lonely white tomboy. After that, Ethel sang only occasionally in clubs and theaters.

Mahalia Jackson, who would rise from anonymity in Chicago to become the world's greatest gospel singer, admired Ethel's gifts. "Ella, Billie, Sarah—they all come from Ethel Waters," Mahalia said about Ethel's influence on the generation of jazz singers to follow.[1] These singers would dominate the art of jazz singing for nearly the rest of the twentieth century. Not only women but many budding male singing stars, such as Joe Williams and Mel Tormé in Chicago, listened to Waters's records for her beautiful voice and story-telling mastery. They worshipped the way she enunciated words.

Some Elements of Song

Ethel, Bing, and all the other successful singers realized early in their careers that the words were as important to them as the music. When they talk about qualities essential to a jazz or a jazz-influenced singer, they mention phrasing (the way the singer puts the words together to tell a story); pronunciation (the accent of the words); and enunciation (the ability to sing the words clearly and meaningfully at any tempo). Words are the building blocks of stories, and every vowel and consonant is important.

Also essential are intonation (the ability to sing in tune at all times); improvisation (the ability to invent original musical phrases); rhythm (the singer's handling of the beat); and the singer's imaginative use of all of the components of a written song. All these elements add up to a singer's ability to challenge, answer, and lead the instruments. Another important element is a singer's vibrato, or quaver in the voice, and the knowledge of when to use it. Countless little touches make up the total sound and approach, or conception, of singers and their ability to elicit an audience's reaction. Singers must also use good arrangements, pace a performance to include slow ballads as well as up-tempo songs, and know what tempos to set. They must decide when to sing and when to use silence for dramatic effect.

A singer's choice of songs affects artistic success enormously. There are few hard and fast rules, however, about material. A good singer can take a terrible song and perform it so well that it becomes an international commercial hit—though it might never become a good song with interesting harmonies. For any singer, the main point is to communicate the song, whether it's a bouncy novelty tune or a lament about love. The best singers make their songs sound like fascinating conversations. "Oh, jazz and love are the hardest things to describe from rationale," Mel Tormé would say long after he had become acknowledged as one of the greatest jazz singers. "Everything you do depends on the kind of song you're singing."[2]

Chapter Four The Big-Band Era Gets into Full Swing

Public events always influence the arts and culture. Franklin Delano Roosevelt became U.S. president, and the nation's economy began to recover slowly from the Great Depression. As if to salute a new era, musicians started swinging hard in big groups with excellent arrangements of songs in the mid-1930s.

That's what people wanted to hear. They held marathon dance contests to this music, too, that could last for days. Anita O'Day danced in those contests before she became a big-band singer with drummer Gene Krupa's group in Chicago in the 1930s. The contests ended by the mid-1930s, but the big bands that dancers loved remained popular entertainment. The big-band era lasted until the late 1940s.

All the bands had singers. They bridged the gap between the abstract, pretty melodies of instrumentalists and the dancers' hunger for mood-lifters and romantic ideas. The bands often had great musicians and fine arrangements. But the singers added drama, glamour, and romance with their individualistic sounds and interpretations of lyrics. Some singers were so good and smart that they went on to greater successes after the bands broke up.

The most important of the swing-band leaders was clarinetist Benny Goodman. Originally from Chicago, he heard Louis Armstrong playing in the South Side's African-American clubs and theaters in the 1920s. Learning from Armstrong and his colleagues, as well as from the wealth of white popular and classical musicians and compositions, Goodman began recording with African-Americans for Columbia and playing with them in concerts in the 1930s. He was the first bandleader to integrate ensembles. He called attention to their talent and creative genius, and he was able to help popularize their exciting, swinging music on a national level.

While the blues dominated popular music in Chicago, Kansas City became a magnet for traveling bandleaders and jazz musicians when clubs opened there in the 1930s. A corrupt political machine run by a man named Boss Pendergast made sure Kansas City was alluring—he kept the illegal liquor flowing during Prohibition in the 1930s. Gamblers and gangsters, along with well-heeled, high-living Midwesterners on vacation, flocked to the paradise of the Kansas City saloons and gambling houses. Management threw in some music, reckoning it as part of the overhead. Musicians weren't well paid, but the atmosphere inspired them. All day and night, they could hear some of the most talented people.

A pianist named William Basie, who was nicknamed the Count, arrived in Kansas City in the 1930s. Originally from Red Bank, New Jersey, he had worked in New York City with great stride piano players; he took lessons from Fats Waller, for example. Stride pianists played melody, harmony, and rhythm all at once. Basie eventually made his way to Kansas City and started leading his own little band.

Other bands traveled through town, among them Andy Kirk and His Clouds of Joy. Kirk had a Kansas City–born ballad singer, Pha Terrell, who became popular for his recordings with the band. Pha (pronounced Fay) had a sweet baritone; he liked to embellish his songs with fancy little trills. His sound and style gave no hint of his beginnings as a tough bouncer in a club.

Another Kansas City–born singer, Joe Turner, shouted the blues in the city's clubs, playing with Albert Ammons and Meade Lux Lewis, a great piano duo of the era. Everyone loved to listen to Joe Turner. Though he could neither read nor write English or music, he composed melodies and lyrics that told strong stories. One of his best, grittiest songs was "Cherry Red," about his love for a married woman with a big brass bed—he liked to roll around in that bed with her until his face turned "Cherry Red," he shouted, even though he knew he was risking his life by having a romance with her. Turner was a huge man with such a robust baritone and physical stamina that he could sing all night without a microphone.

Another blues singer in the Kansas City clubs, Jimmy Rushing, originally from Oklahoma, had a higher-pitched, more plaintive sound than Turner's. He performed with the Basie band. The bands broadcast live on the radio, and on shortwave bands they could be heard in distant cities. Benny Goodman tuned in the Basie band on the radio in Chicago and told his friend and mentor, record producer John Hammond. Hammond listened to Basie and hurried to Kansas City to sign him to a contract for tours and records. Jimmy Rushing was hired to sing the blues on Basie's first records.

They went south first. Jimmy Rushing's singing attracted crowds for Basie's musicians. Then Basie, Rushing, and the band traveled to New York. Basie went on to international fame and fortune, and he almost always featured a singer who could perform his swinging, blues-based music.

When Prohibition was repealed and drinking again became legal, the Pendergast machine lost its influence. The hot, swinging music of the

Big Joe Turner's voice filled the nights in Kansas City jazz clubs during the 1930s, when the Pendergast machine ruled the city. Big Joe composed songs and sang sophisticated urban blues, influencing many rising jazz singers. Here he is as a young man in 1939.

nights gravitated eastward to undisputed headquarters in New York City. With their distinctive, recognizable sounds and theme songs, the band singers and instrumentalists attracted fans by performing in New York hotel dining rooms and ballrooms. Radios broadcast the music all around the country; these broadcasts were called remotes. Every big city, and many small ones, had ballrooms, theaters, and hotels, where bands played on their tours. People turned out in droves to dance in person to the music they had fallen in love with on the radio broadcasts.

The movie industry in Los Angeles also attracted musicians and singers. Los Angeles had many theaters and a lively nightlife in clubs. But New York had even more. Musicians and singers regarded it as the top of the pile. They nicknamed it the Big Apple.

Some bands played swinging music, and others were known for having sweet sounds. Most bands had a "girl singer" and a "boy singer"; some had one singer for the blues and another for ballads. Singers had to fit in with the characteristic sounds of the bands that hired them. Leaders could be sensitive to the talents of their singers and had excellent arrangements written especially for them. Those singers were the lucky ones. They blossomed under such encouraging conditions. Other singers had to use arrangements done with the instrumentalists or other singers in mind.

It was not easy to be a band singer. Unlike instrumentalists, singers didn't belong to unions. Without that protection, they tried to do extra jobs behind the scenes to make their jobs secure. They carried music books and ran errands for leaders and instrumentalists. During performances, they had to stand in front of the band and sound wonderful all the time. If they sang a wrong note, they had no way to hide it. So singers got reputations for being temperamental and nervous, even though many were not. Along with all the pressures of performing, they had to look great, too; after hours on a tour bus, a singer had to look fresh and have clothes that were clean and pressed.

Bands could travel as much as five hundred miles from one job to the next. Tour buses were little convoys hurtling through lonesome countrysides in the wee hours of the mornings. To stay healthy, band members learned to sleep sitting up in their seats. When they weren't sleeping, they played cards, read, or talked. The buses were like tiny mobile towns, and bands were little families. Some became fond of each other and helped each other through the lonely nights away from home. Others had fights. Some singers changed bands two or more times during their careers and became more prominent with each change. Still others carried on romances; many singers married their bandleaders.

The list of singers who became well known with the most popular bands is very long. Among those whose fame would outlive the bands are Frank Sinatra and Jo Stafford with Tommy Dorsey's band. Tommy's brother, Jimmy, had a band, too, with his own singers, including Helen O'Connell. She never thought of herself as a jazz singer, though she was definitely jazz-influenced. The Dorseys had two of the most famous bands of the era.

Ella Fitzgerald began as a teenager with drummer-bandleader Chick Webb. Helen Ward, Martha Tilton, Helen Forrest, and then Peggy Lee sang with bandleader Benny Goodman, who was billed as the "King of Swing." Peggy, with her pretty, round face and blonde hair was a show-stopper on looks alone. Her style conveyed the intimacy of a long, loving kiss. Her tone was warm, her intonation exquisite, her rhythmic feeling as strong a pulse as a bass fiddle's. And she knew exactly how to deliver lyrics to hold an audience rapt. She wrote a big hit, "Why Don't You Do Right?", which she sang with the band. After the big-band era, she went on to have hits on her own, such as "Fever" and "Lover."

Perry Como, the singer with the Ted Weems band, had a smooth and lyrical voice, and he was inspired, as so many "boy singers" were, by the relaxed sound of Bing Crosby. After the big-band era, singers such as Vic Damone patterned themselves after both Crosby and Como.

Helen Forrest, a white woman, took over Billie Holiday's job with Artie Shaw's band when it became too difficult for Billie to keep working with a white band under the conditions of segregation. Billie had been one of the first African-American singers to travel with a white band. Dick Haymes, whose wonderful voice seemed influenced by Crosby's style, cut a swath through the 1940s and 1950s. One of his early jobs was with Artie Shaw.

Helen Forrest also worked with Benny Goodman and then became more popular with trumpeter Harry James's band. He had his biggest hits because of Helen. Rosemary Clooney worked with bandleader Tony Pastor before she became an internationally famous recording star in the 1950s. Ivie Anderson was best known for singing with Duke Ellington. Of Ellington's many wonderful band singers, Ivie had one of the most distinguished styles. Anita O'Day first won respect for her work with bandleader Gene Krupa, a drummer. She made classic recordings with him and his star trumpeter, Roy Eldridge, before she went to star with Stan Kenton's band.

Cab Calloway's band featured his own strong, borderline tenor-baritone voice. Raised in Baltimore, Maryland, Cab followed his sister to Chicago during the 1920s. He had promised his parents that he would go to law school, but his sister Blanche, a gifted singer, found him a job in a show. After that, he couldn't keep himself away from show business. Soon he was leading a band and singing in South Side clubs. As the musical freshness and momentum began to leave Chicago, Cab brought a band to New York, where he didn't fare well at first. His band simply couldn't play as well as the big, slick swing bands there. Then he took over another band that had a lackluster leader. Soon Cab was a major attraction at the Cotton Club.

He became known as the "hi-de-ho man" for singing that phrase in a song that became associated with him forever: "Minnie the Moocher," about a sexy hoochie kooch dancer. His band was filled with excellent musicians. But it was Cab, with his long, dark hair flying around, that caused the most excitement. His luxuriously draped white formal tails billowed gracefully as he twisted and danced. When he went on the road, the band earned so much money that the men had to hide it by stuffing it in the bass fiddle and the drum heads. Cab's band, one of the

Swingers and Crooners

most famous in the 1930s, lasted until 1947.

Johnny Desmond, in the Crosby tradition, sang with Krupa, too, and with Glenn Miller, a very popular band leader during World War II. Miller died in an airplane crash, on his way to Europe to entertain American troops. But his band had so many fans that it kept going without him. It also had heroic status because its leader was killed in the war. Merv Griffin sang with Freddy Martin's band before he became famous as a television talk show host.

Chris Connor and June Christy, modeling themselves after Anita O'Day, sang with Stan Kenton's band; the band tried to use some of the coming innovations in jazz that would become known as bebop. Though Billie Holiday didn't record with the big bands she traveled with, she went on the road with Count Basie in 1938, along with Jimmy Rushing, and the next year she worked with Artie Shaw. Lena Horne worked with the composer and bandleader Noble Sissle before she became one of the first African-American "girl singers" to work with a white swing band. It was led by saxophonist Charlie Barnet.

In the 1940s, when they were very young, Dinah Washington and Betty Carter traveled with Lionel Hampton's band. A vibes player and drummer, "Hamp" also did a little singing. Clarinetist Woody Herman sang with his own band. And some bandleaders had musicians who "doubled" as singers. Alto saxophonist Earl Warren, for one, sang his own song "Poor Little Plaything" with Count Basie's band.

Dinah Washington began as a gospel singer and went on to become a pop star in her own right, spawning many imitators by the 1950s, among them Nancy Wilson, Dakota Staton, and Eartha Kitt. Dinah could sing the blues, and pop, and jazz improvisations. Above all, with her powerful, soulful, gospel-rooted style, she established standards for the rhythm and blues singers who dominated pop music in the late 1960s. Aretha Franklin, who also began by singing gospel and playing piano and organ in Baptist churches, loved Dinah. By the 1970s, Natalie Cole, a virtual disciple of Aretha, developed an affinity for both gospel and rhythm and blues. And Bette Midler became a soulful pop singer after imbibing Dinah Washington's influence.

Betty Carter was a maverick. She would travel a very long, rough road on her way to becoming a star, because she decided to sing progressive, experimental songs. But she started in the swing era, singing bebop at bandleader Lionel Hampton's request. He called her "Betty Bebop."

Pretty, blonde Doris Day, with a soft, seductive voice and an especially intimate sound, worked with bandleader Les Brown. Harriet Hilliard played with her husband Ozzie Nelson's band. Betty Hutton sang with Vincent Lopez. These three singers went on to become famous in Hollywood. Doris and Betty were cast as romantic leading ladies in blockbuster Technicolor movies with famous leading men. Though Harriet Hilliard had the potential to become a big star, she didn't get along well enough with a major film studio's head, and she found herself bypassed for important roles. She became known instead for her radio show with her husband, Ozzie.

Lena Horne married arranger Lenny Hayton, a white man, in 1947. She would later reveal that she felt insulted because of the way African-Americans were treated in Hollywood, often cast in demeaning roles or scenes that could be cut when the movies played in the South. Over the years, she developed into an important jazz singing star because of the techniques and polish she acquired from listening to the great musicians her husband introduced her to.

In a variation on that theme, singer Pearl Bailey, who sang with Cootie Williams's orchestra, married a white drummer, Louis Bellson, in 1952. Their interracial marriage made headlines in the newspapers. Bellson worked with Duke Ellington's orchestra. But it was Pearl, a few years older than Louis, who overrode prejudices with her relaxed, outgoing, witty personality.

She was so relaxed onstage that she seemed not to have to take singing very seriously at all. She was thoroughly unconcerned about glamour and success. She also had such wit, intelligence, and poise that she made lasting friendships with the influential people she met. She became an adviser to presidents of the United States and was chosen as a United Nations representative for the United States. She went to school for graduate degrees, wrote books about her life and philosophy, and still performed from time to time. No other singer became as prominent in public life as Pearl. Her life bore testimony to the power of the individual will.

After World War II, most big bands broke up for financial reasons. The instrumentalists headed to New York City, looking for jobs in the recording studios. Instead of suffering from the demise of the big bands, many singers with well-rounded voices and talents were thrilled to discover they could become stars on their own, making records in studios and traveling with their own smaller groups.

The economic reasons for the demise of the big-band era and the rise of singers on their own usually had little to do with the musical quality of the bands. Until 1942, the bands were in demand everywhere. But at the end of 1942, the American Federation of Musicians —the musicians' union—launched a strike against recording companies in an attempt to get them to pay royalties to the union and to provide better working conditions for musicians. The strike lasted until early 1944. During the strike, singers made recordings without instrumental accompaniment, sometimes backed up only by vocal choruses. Those were the war years, too. The public longed to hear the characteristic sounds of the singers, with their cheerful or sentimental songs. They kept up everyone's spirits. And the bands lost some of their members, even bandleaders, to the draft.

When the strike was over, bandleaders faced the rising costs of transporting bands around the country. Also, musicians during the war had begun to work in little groups. These small combos became quite popular with the public. The big bands never recovered their dominant position in music. In 1946 and 1947, several important bands folded.

Record companies now depended on the popularity of singers to lead the way to the top of the charts. In comparison to the way they had once lived on the road, missing meals and taking abuse from some instrumentalists, singers were now virtually coddled in the studios. Record companies tried to find them the best new songs. When there was a happy marriage between a singer and a song, everyone involved reaped great financial rewards—at least, record companies and singers did. Instrumentalists earned fees dictated by union requirements—good fees but not necessarily as impressive as the money singers earned from royalties for their hit records. By the late 1940s, the golden age of singers had begun.

Chapter Five Stars from the Big-Band Era

The big bands had been almost completely segregated. Musicians did not want it that way, but segregation was either the custom or the law in many parts of the United States. Musicians of different races often weren't allowed to work on the same stage simultaneously.

On rare occasions, white bandleaders hired African-American musicians, singers, and arrangers, and tried to get around the segregation laws. A few African-American bandleaders did the same thing. And musicians and singers of all backgrounds learned techniques from each other. Despite some instances of tension, there were more interracial friendships and professional collaborations behind the scenes in the jazz world than in any other part of society. And everyone in the music world recognized the genius of Billie Holiday.

Billie Holiday

Billie was one of the greatest jazz singers in history. Since her death in 1959, at the age of forty-four, her recordings have been reissued countless times. A collection released in 1993 won a Grammy award. She has also been written about more than any other jazz singer in history, not because of her great artistry but because she lived a reckless life filled with scandals. A cult of "Lady Day," as she was nicknamed, keeps growing.[1]

Billie had a mysterious sound. When she was young, her voice was nearly clear and high-pitched. Throughout her life it remained arresting, because of its unusual timbre and her slow, drawled phrasing. Almost unique among singers, she used a whine instead of a growl to express pain or passion. She improvised melodies so deftly it was impossible to analyze exactly how she did it. She used tones between notes, and the tones suggested that the melodies were about to go in surprising directions. She could suggest more emotion with one bent note or tone than other people could communicate with a dozen notes. The very thing that she was most famous for—laying back on the beat, or singing behind the beat until she decided to catch up with it—caused her the most trouble commercially.

Some club owners, in the 1930s, yelled at her to sing faster and louder or get out. She told them to sing their way and she would sing her way. She got out of their clubs, but never peaceably. Sometimes she threw their furniture around their offices on her way out the door. In short, she refused to change the way she sang.

Although she didn't sing as many blues as ballads, she was thought of as a bluesy singer because of the plaintive quality of her voice. She did sing some famous blues, among them "Fine and Mellow," "Billie's Blues," and "Travelin' Light," the last about traveling through life without a man. She always became involved with sharp-looking hustlers who treated her badly. The relationships didn't last long, and they usually did her more harm than good. She became a drug addict during her first, brief marriage to a drug user.

Call Billie's work a monotone with a bounce. Or call it a dreamy reverie, or a lazy sounding conversation with a hint of a contented cat's purr. John Hammond, who discovered her in a Harlem club and was the first to record her, said the sound of her voice was the greatest non-classical vocalizing on records. Her range was less than two octaves, but her small voice was as effective as that of any impassioned, shouting soul singer.

Billie led a difficult life. Her body was bruised and battered by heroin, alcohol, cigarettes, and physical fights. Techniques—such as capturing the sound of laughter by hitting staccato notes and gliding on them—survived as a cloak, a showy wardrobe for her ruined vocal instrument. Her odd sound became even odder, her high voice even more eerie in its pitch. It lost the buoyancy of her young, healthy days. But her sound still haunted audiences.

Billie was born Eleanora Fagan in 1915 in Philadelphia, where her mother, Sadie Fagan, worked as a maid. Soon they returned to her mother's native Baltimore, where Billie's father lived. Clarence Holiday, a budding big-band guitarist, visited her occasionally but took no responsibility for her.

Her mother often left town to work for the higher wages offered maids in the North, leaving Billie in the care of unkind relatives. When Sadie and Billie lived together, their lives were unsettled because they were so poor, and Sadie herself had troubled relationships with men. Billie enjoyed an affectionate relationship with a very old great-grandmother, who, some say, died in her arms.

The luckiest thing that happened to Billie early in her life was her discovery of recordings by Louis Armstrong and Bessie Smith. Billie started to learn about singing from them. As a young teenager, she probably worked as a prostitute. She liked the slick characters she met. They gave her tips, and they reminded her of her father, who also loved to hang out with fast company at night. She used the money to go to the movies, and she decided to take the name Billie in honor of her favorite actress, Billie Dove.

By her early teens, she was living with her mother in New York City and singing in Queens, Brooklyn, and Harlem. John Hammond heard her in a Harlem club and arranged her first recording date in 1933, with a group that included Benny Goodman. Their songs were "Riffing the Scotch" and "Your Mother's Son-in-Law," which are often reissued in collections today. She was booked to play at the Apollo Theater. A writer described her impact: "The sight of this tall, buxom, beautiful girl with the exquisite coloring was enough to make any neck swivel. On looks alone, Billie was potential star material, but her voice was her greatest asset, for she sang in a style that was new to the world."[2]

In 1938, she went on the road to sing ballads with Basie's band. Jimmy Rushing sang the blues. Band members loved her singing and her sense of camaraderie. But she was signed to Columbia, and Basie had a contract with another company; she could not record with the band. Trumpeter Buck Clayton thought Billie was fired from the band late in 1938 because of a never-explained disagreement with Basie about money. Also, Billie could be moody. John Hammond, who still had a connection to the Basie band management, may have wanted Billie out of the band. Basie said about her, "Billie is a marvelous artist who remains unappreciated by the world at large."[3] Billie and Basie remained friends, and they performed together again years later.

She began recording in a group with pianist Teddy Wilson, who had a light, articulate touch, and in 1939 she led her own groups for Columbia's race records division. In her groups were her great friends tenor saxophonist Lester Young and trumpeter Buck Clayton, who played in Count Basie's band. Billie and Lester were known for sharing a soft-toned, languid style that made people think of them as musical soulmates. Lester nicknamed her "Lady Day," and she dubbed him "Prez," the president of the tenor saxophone.

Billie Holiday posed with friends for a photo behind Harlem's Apollo Theater in August 1935, including the great tenor saxophonist Ben Webster (left) and pianist Roger "Ram" Ramirez (kneeling in front); Ram wrote "Lover Man," Billie's greatest commercial hit on records.

In 1939, Billie took the brave step of joining Artie Shaw's band; it had only one African-American instrumentalist at the time. Though she and Artie fought vigorously against acts of prejudice, occasionally he had to give in to pressures or give up bookings. He hired a second singer, Helen Forrest, a white woman, to come along, too. In her autobiography, Billie wrote, "It wasn't long before the roughest days with the Basie band began to look like a breeze. I got to the point where I hardly ever ate, slept or went to the bathroom without having a major NAACP type production."[4]

Helen observed Billie's torment: "It was so much easier for me just because I was white. I envied her singing, if not her life." The job with Shaw helped Helen overcome memories of her own terrible childhood. Billie's experiences remained depressing. "Lady Day was a lady with a lot of dignity," Helen said. "But white audiences saw only her color and didn't hear her singing."[5]

Billie quit the band when a New York hotel didn't allow her to sing at all. Soon she was starring on 52nd Street at the Onyx and other clubs. Then she sang for the opening of Barney Josephson's new club, Cafe Society Downtown, in New York's Greenwich Village, where patrons of all races, some of them wealthy, mingled freely in the audience. Billie hit her stride there. Josephson thought she gained confidence because of his insistence on total integration. Her fame spread.

Josephson handed her a dramatic anti-lynching song called "Strange Fruit," written by a friend of his. The song title refers to lynching victims hanging from trees. Billie thought it over and decided that she was a "race woman," even though she was not a civil rights battler.[6] She agreed to sing the song. She performed on a darkened stage with one spotlight on her face. Audiences were shocked at first; then they applauded wildly. Columbia would not record "Strange Fruit," so she got the Commodore label, headed by Milt Gabler, to do it. Almost no one but Billie has ever sung "Strange Fruit"; it was always considered her song.

Though Billie's career brightened, her life story darkened—she became a heroin addict. "I had the white gown and the white shoes, and every night they'd bring me the white gardenias and the white junk," she said.[7] She checked into a hospital, where her manager persuaded her to quit her habit. Once the police found out she had gone for a cure, they discovered her habit and followed her everywhere. The cure didn't last. In 1947, she was sent to jail for nine months on a drug possession charge. It's a measure of how depressed she was that she didn't sing a note there.

Right after she came out, she performed a comeback concert at Carnegie Hall. It was so crowded that some people sat on the stage. She couldn't follow up that triumph with club dates, because she had lost her New York cabaret card due to the arrest—police did not issue cards to people convicted of felonies. She was never legally able to perform in a New York club again. To make matters worse, she went back to drugs.

In the 1940s, Billie had complained about never having won a *Down Beat* magazine poll. So beleaguered was she that in 1950 *Down Beat* called her "Lady Yesterday." But in 1954, it turned around completely and gave her an award as "one of the all-time great vocalists in jazz."[8]

In the 1950s, signed to record for Verve, she traveled around the world. Even though her voice deteriorated year by year, she was still Lady Day, a favorite with audiences. In 1957, she signed a new contract with Columbia, which led to her appearance in a television series called "The Seven Lively Arts." Her version of the blues tune "Fine and Mellow" became a jazz world classic. She sang in ecstatic communion with legendary instrumentalists, including Lester Young. Her luminous eyes stayed riveted upon him; her head nodded with rhythmic feeling. The performance became available on a video called *The Sound Of Jazz*, one of the most famous jazz films.

In 1958, she recorded an album with strings, *Lady in Satin*, on which she sounded hoarse and world-weary—yet somehow still fascinating. Her body kept weakening. In 1959, she collapsed and was hospitalized for several illnesses. Officially, she died of kidney failure. One musician would always recall that a neighbor in Greenwich Village, hearing of Billie's death, played Billie's recording of the blues song "Gloomy Sunday" over and over again.

During her short life, the popularity of the blues and Dixieland had given way to the swing era. Then the swing era was upstaged by the embellishments of a band of revolutionary jazz musicians, the beboppers, who began to spread their style around in the 1940s. But Billie hadn't needed to alter her style to attract audiences. Instrumentalists as well as singers learned from her records. Her voice had a timeless, lighter-than-air musicality. Singer Sylvia Syms, who worshipped Billie and stood outside 52nd Street clubs when she was too young to go inside and hear Billie in person, said, "From listening to her I realized that the goal was to relate things to people who are listening to you and not to lose sight of your story and what it means to you."[9]

Ella Fitzgerald

When Billie Holiday was making her first recordings, fifteen-year-old Ella Fitzgerald started working with a well-known, swinging band in Harlem. It was led by drummer Chick Webb, who was looking for a girl to sing up-tempo tunes. One of his bandmembers brought Ella to meet him backstage at the Apollo Theater. Chick almost didn't hire her, because she was dirty and dressed in rags and men's shoes. She had been living by her wits on the streets in Harlem, dancing and singing for pennies, running numbers, and doing other odd jobs.

Ella was born in Newport News, Virginia, in 1918. She spent her childhood with her mother, stepfather, and half sister in Yonkers, New York, and dreamed of becoming a dancer. At home she sang along with Connee Boswell records bought by her mother. Then her mother died. An aunt rescued her from an abusive stepfather and took her to live in Harlem. But Ella was caught playing hooky from school and was sent to live in an institution. She ran away to live in the streets. When she entered the Apollo Theater amateur contest and won, she expected she would get the normal prize—a week's work at the theater. But she looked so ragged and neglected that the theater didn't let her work.

That's when Chick Webb found her, bought her a dress, and took her with his band to play a dance at Yale University. If the kids liked her, he said, that was all that mattered. They loved her. Somehow, from listening to her idol, Connee Boswell—a white singer in the Boswell Sisters group that sang in tight harmony—Ella had trained herself to swing hard, with an energetic, nimble, girlish, bell-like voice.

In the late 1930s, she scored a big hit with a tune she wrote herself, "A Tisket, A Tasket." Under the protection of Chick and his wife, Ella blossomed into a popular, sunny-sounding, rhythmically brilliant novelty and ballad singer. She never sang the blues. Once she got onstage and opened her mouth, every problem in the world evaporated for herself and her audiences.

Chick Webb died in 1939, bequeathing his band to Ella. Musicians helped her keep it going. In 1940, she hired trumpeter Dizzy Gillespie, who had just been fired from the Cab Calloway band. Dizzy had cut Cab with a knife during a fight, and everyone became frightened of him. He was grateful to Ella and her band for hiring him when he needed work so badly.

Then her musicians were drafted for World War II. She was reduced to leading a small group called Ella Fitzgerald and the Four Keys. That, too, was cut down to a skeleton. Ella went solo. At this time, against the advice of musicians who were her friends, she married a shipyard worker named Benny Kornegay on a dare; she soon had the marriage annulled. She had a recording contract with Decca, a good company, and she had some hits. But her career lacked good management. Picking some of her own songs by instinct, she managed to fill the 1940s and early 1950s with good songs and novelty tunes done with orchestras, including strings.

Ella Fitzgerald toured in the late 1940s with a small bebop group led by Dizzy Gillespie (right), when she was developing her peerless scat style. She married the band's bassist, Ray Brown Sr. (left). Vibist Milt Jackson (far right) is behind Dizzy.

Swingers and Crooners

Dizzy Gillespie returned a favor when he hired her to sing with his band in the 1940s. Always shy and overweight, with no taste for alcohol or cigarettes, she didn't socialize with the men in his band. Her only vice was overeating. Dizzy encouraged her to try to sing progressive jazz—bebop—and keep up with the changing times. That's when she started scatting—singing those old "monkey shine" nonsense words, as Danny Barker called them—which suited the fast, adventurous music being played by Dizzy's band. Her style became more exciting. She had a big hit with "How High the Moon," scatting with her peerless sense of rhythm that allowed her to move like quicksilver over the notes, perfectly in tune.

In Dizzy's band, she met and married Ray Brown, a talented bassist several years younger than she. When Ella left Dizzy, Ray went with her and played for her group. Ella still needed a good manager. One night, as she sat in at a concert where Ray Brown was playing, a brilliant entrepreneur named Norman Granz listened to her carefully. The concert was part of his Jazz at the Philharmonic series. He noticed how much his audience liked Ella's singing. Gradually she started working for Granz's productions.

Ray Brown was offered a chance to play in pianist Oscar Peterson's trio. Ray yearned to accept the challenge. Ella wanted him to remain as her accompanist and revolve around her career. They had adopted a child—her half sister's son—and named him Ray Brown Jr. But they couldn't hold their marriage together. Their high-powered careers took them in different directions. Ray Sr. went off to become one of the most renowned jazz bassists in the world; young bassists revered him as much as singers idolized Ella.

By 1955, Ella's relationship with Norman Granz had grown secure. He manipulated Decca to free Ella from her contract. She then signed with Granz's label, Verve. For Decca, she had done one album of George Gershwin's music. Under Granz's wing, she began recording albums of all the most famous American composers—Cole Porter,

Jerome Kern, Johnny Mercer, Rodgers and Hart, Harold Arlen, Irving Berlin, Duke Ellington, W. C. Handy—and many of the albums became hits. In Granz she found a great guide. Her career soared above almost everyone else's, man or woman, singer or instrumentalist. She won more than a dozen Grammy awards and sold so many albums that she and Granz became millionaires.

She sang in every important hall and theater in the world for the rest of her life, working so hard—sometimes flying from one city to another to give two concerts in one night—that in middle age she became exhausted. She collapsed several times. When she sang with other singers, she eclipsed them completely. Frank Sinatra, among others, had to sing his heart out just to keep up with her. She became America's sweetheart of popular jazz singing. As a rhythm singer, nobody ever beat her. She could sing ballads, too, with a beautiful voice, and she could give such an affecting reading of some lyrics that she and Sarah Vaughan shared honors as the two greatest pop-jazz singers who ever lived. But Ella, whose voice was less glorious than Sarah's, had greater commercial appeal. She became better known and was the highest paid singing star in jazz.

She was also the most reclusive. When a show was over, she retreated to her hotel room with her cousin, who was hired as her maid and traveling companion. Or she went to her house in Beverly Hills. She had a few romances, but they failed to offer her love and companionship. She told a writer that it was impossible for her to live on the road and find the time to build a relationship with a husband. She felt very sorry about that. Musicians who traveled with her thought she lived a lonely life.[10] At the same time they could not believe the energy she had to keep working so constantly. Some quit her group because they couldn't stand the pace.

One of her accompanists, pianist Jimmy Rowles, understood that she focused completely on music. That was her whole life. "When she walks down the street, she leaves a trail of notes," he explained.[11]

Jo Stafford

Virtually overnight, Jo Stafford went from starvation with an octet of singers to stardom with Tommy Dorsey's dance band. Born in 1917 in California, Jo fell in love with Benny Goodman's saxophone section and Duke Ellington's whole band. She and other members of her high school's glee club chipped in five cents each and bought Duke's record of "Sophisticated Lady." When an earthquake wrecked her high school in Long Beach, California, in 1933, she attended classes held in tents. Every morning before school started, she got together with friends and listened to Duke's record in a tent. Jo also liked listening to Ella Fitzgerald records.

In her teens, Jo sang with her sisters in a trio, then joined an octet called the Pied Pipers. Other musicians liked them. Alice King, who performed in a family singing group, the King Sisters, heard the Pied Pipers performing in Los Angeles. She told her boyfriend, a young arranger named Paul Weston. Alice's sister Yvonne also told her boyfriend, arranger Axel Stordahl. Axel and Paul, who worked in Tommy Dorsey's band, told Dorsey. When he took his band to play in the Palomar Ballroom in Los Angeles, Dorsey auditioned the Pied Pipers and hired them to sing with his band on a radio show. But eight singers turned out to be too expensive for Dorsey. He had to fire them. The Pied Pipers went from riches to rags. Four of them quit the group.

Then in December of 1939, Dorsey called Jo from Chicago and asked her to bring a quartet to play with him at the Palmer House. With her silky voice, Jo was the group's lead singer, then a soloist. Critics noticed, too, that she had a blue, sad sound that made her stand out from most other singers. She couldn't explain why she sounded blue, or even cool, but the public loved her mysterious sound. She got fan letters from soldiers fighting in World War II. "They talked about my haunting quality. They said it made them homesick and happy to be unhappy. . . . It made them lonesome for their girlfriends," she told a writer years later.[12]

Unlike most singers, she was delighted by her life on the road with a big band. The pace was tiring, but she loved the camaraderie with musicians, who talked, joked, and sympathized with each other's problems. A skinny young singer named Frank Sinatra joined Dorsey's band while Jo was singing with it. "He was one of the best of all time," she recalled about Sinatra. He would mature into one of the century's most important and legendary pop-jazz singers. "The first time I heard him, I knew it. Before him, everyone tried to sound like Crosby. But no one has sounded like Sinatra before or since."[13]

Johnny Mercer, a composer and singer who taught Jo about the lightness and humor in jazz singing, founded a new recording company, Capitol, in 1942. When she left the Dorsey band that year, Mercer signed her to Capitol. Her records became very popular. In 1951, she went on to record for Columbia. The next year she married Paul Weston, the arranger who had originally recommended her to Dorsey. With a happy marriage, two children, and a career that had outlasted the big-band era, she lost that blue tinge in her voice. She stopped performing in 1959.

Frank Sinatra

In 1937, Frank Sinatra, that skinny kid from Hoboken, New Jersey, landed a job at the Rustic Cabin roadhouse in Englewood, New Jersey, as singer in the band and as head waiter. The Rustic Cabin had a hookup with radio. One night, trumpeter-bandleader Harry James, lying in bed in New York, tuned in his radio and heard Sinatra. Harry was only twenty in 1938 when he started his band; he had been playing in bands, including Glenn Miller's and Benny Goodman's, since he was thirteen. Life was a struggle, but he was playing at the Paramount Theater in New York, and he wanted the young singer he heard on the radio to sing with his band. By mid-1939, Sinatra made his first recordings with the James

Masterful jazz singer Frank "the Chairman of the Board" Sinatra is shown here with bandleader/trombonist Tommy Dorsey at the popular Hotel Astor in New York City in 1941. Sinatra said he learned phrasing from watching Dorsey's breathing technique.

band. Although he had a cocky personality offstage, Sinatra wasn't brimming with self-confidence onstage. Critics noticed he seemed unsure of himself. But he had a pleasant voice and a talent for phrasing lyrics in an appealing way.[14] He convinced audiences of his sincerity.

On the road, Harry James's band ran into financial difficulties. It didn't play softly enough to suit some restaurant owners. James had a beautiful tone, but his style was showy, brassy, and loud. In Chicago, when Tommy Dorsey's band was booked at the Sherman House, Dorsey went to hear James and loved Sinatra's singing. Dorsey offered Frank a job. Frank asked James for permission to get out of his contract, and James agreed, knowing that Sinatra and his wife, Nancy, were soon going to have their first baby. He and Sinatra remained friends forever, and occasionally worked together again. Sinatra then went to work with the more established Dorsey band—a great opportunity.

Sinatra replaced a very popular singer named Jack Leonard. Everyone wondered if Sinatra would let the band down. But from his debut with Dorsey, Sinatra excited audiences so much they yelled for him to sing more. By the time he got to the Paramount Theater in New York, every newspaper was printing stories about him. His name was becoming a household word.

Sinatra learned how to breathe correctly by watching the way Dorsey played trombone. Sinatra later praised Dorsey for teaching him about phrasing and giving him overall musical knowledge.[15] Then Sinatra wanted to get out of his contract with Dorsey and go out on his own. That's how popular Frank had become. Dorsey didn't want him to leave. They fought so bitterly that they never reconciled. The story surfaced (in a 1990s television movie about Sinatra's life) that Dorsey had charged Sinatra a percentage of his future earnings as the price of letting the singer out of his contract. It took years before that arrangement was changed. Then Frank was truly free.

Sinatra endured one of the most turbulent careers in American popular music. For a while after leaving Dorsey, he continued as a bobby-soxer's idol with a clean image. He settled in Hollywood with his wife and children. But he upset the public in the 1950s when he had a scandalous romance with actress Ava Gardner. In those days, the public didn't forgive stars who committed adultery. The love affair broke up his marriage. Eventually he married Ava Gardner—but not before his hot temper and brash manner in dealing with reporters earned him very negative headlines. His marriage to Ava was embattled, too. He even punched reporters who wrote about his troubles. His career went on the skids.

Sinatra needed a break to bring him back to prominence. He got that chance when he was given the role of a soldier named Maggio in a movie about World War II, *From Here to Eternity*. It was generally believed that, behind the scenes, the powerful head of a Mafia family terrorized the film's producer into hiring Frankie. The Mafia chief knew Frank's mother, who had political influence in her hometown. Then Sinatra surprised everyone by acting so well that he won an Academy Award as Best Supporting Actor. In the movie he didn't sing a note, but his career as a singer picked up again. Every male singer in the country joked about wanting to play the role of a soldier in a World War II movie. Sinatra became so influential that he earned the nickname "Chairman of the Board."

Back when he was struggling with his career, he had wanted to sign a contract with Capitol Records. The bosses of Capitol actually asked Nat "King" Cole, then a star at the label, what he thought of Sinatra. Nat said they should sign him if they could get him. Sinatra liked working with arranger Nelson Riddle, who was helped out by Cole. Cole had just recorded "Too Young," a big hit, and was asked to do the tune "Young at Heart" next. He generously said, "Give it to Frank."[16] That song became a hit for Sinatra. Riddle wasn't often free to work with Cole anymore, because from then on he was always working with Sinatra.

Sinatra's marriages, romances, and swashbuckling lifestyle contributed to his image as a heavy drinker who loved all-night parties and Nevada gambling casinos. His reputation as a friend of Mafia families cost him a friendship with President John F. Kennedy. But Frank's singing career and style were unaffected. Wherever he sang, his shows were sold out.

He always worked with the best arrangers and musicians in recording studios, theaters, and concert halls, whether in Los Angeles, New York, London, or anyplace else. When most singers took a drink onstage, it was usually water to help soothe their throats. But Sinatra affected the pose of sipping wine. Journalists nicknamed him "Ol' Blue Eyes." He gained weight. Altogether he looked and sounded better in middle age than he had as a skinny kid with a small, wavering high baritone.

Singers have always recognized Sinatra's gift for singing a lyric convincingly. He sounded as if he was telling audiences stories about his life. Anne Marie Moss, a young Canadian singer, began listening to his earliest records, made between 1940 and 1942 with Dorsey. When she heard Sinatra sing "Violets for Your Furs," she imagined seeing sleet for miles around her.[17]

Sinatra's voice lacked the smoothness of Crosby's. Frank was a brash, cool, edgy, and unsentimental modern singer. His voice deepened with age into a true baritone, and he exhibited techniques learned from such diverse sources as Billie Holiday and Mabel Mercer, a British-born singer who worked in fashionable supper clubs. He also picked up techniques from instrumentalists, particularly horn players. His face brimmed with emotion as he sang his arias about real love and whirlwind romances. He could shout an up-tempo song hoarsely, and he could sing a tender ballad softly and slowly. A master of dynamics, he had a perfect sense of when to sing loudly or softly.

He could play tricks with a tempo, speeding it up and slowing it down within a single word.[18] And he could transform himself into the quintessential rogue with his dramatic version of "One for My Baby," when he called for one more drink at nearly three in the morning. He wanted a drink to toast his lover, and another drink to prepare him for his upcoming trip on the highway, or perhaps, for the entire road of life. He never sang about playing it safe.

In short, he could wrap audiences around his little finger and create an atmosphere of suspense, glamour, romance, passion—anything a story called for, anything he wanted.

Dick Haymes

After Sinatra left Harry James, Dick Haymes was hired to demonstrate a composer's songs for James. Haymes caught the bandleader's ear more than the songs did. Though he was Latin in background (born in Buenos Aires, Argentina, in 1916), he had none of that supposed fieriness in his style. His baritone voice was smooth; his intonation was perfect; and his style was natural and quiet. He sang in slow and medium-slow tempos — the speed of good conversation. James hired him. Later Haymes worked for Tommy Dorsey after Sinatra left.

Haymes's long career had its ups and downs, involving his opposition to the draft, unpaid taxes, alcohol, and failed marriages to beautiful women, including movie star Rita Hayworth. But he kept singing through the 1940s and 1950s, with well-known bands. The quality of his moody, romantic ballads endured. With his clean-cut, boyish good looks, an impression which was heightened by his little turned-up nose, he starred as a romantic hero in Hollywood movies. His records are still played on radio shows that feature "golden oldies." More than any other singer, he could sound as if he was truly in love with a woman and pouring his heart out to her, without ever seeming corny.[19] He ranked high in the esteem of jazz aficionados, who admired his technique, beautiful voice, and emotionalism.

Helen Forrest

When Harry James began to hire women singers, his best choice was Helen Forrest, who had received her first break with Artie Shaw's band. Until she got into the Shaw band, Helen had lived a life that rivaled Billie Holiday's for misery. Her stepfather had run a whorehouse in her mother's living room, and Helen had been sexually abused by him. Her mother didn't help her, so Helen ran to her piano teacher's apartment

Helen Forrest and trumpeter/bandleader Harry James had some of their greatest hits together in the 1940s.

and lived there. The teacher encouraged Helen's singing talent and introduced her to the records of Mildred Bailey and Ella Fitzgerald.

Eventually Helen found a permanent gig at a Washington, D.C., club called the Madrillon, where drummer Ziggy Elman heard her. They had known each other as children in Philadelphia. Ziggy recommended her to Artie Shaw. Early in life, Helen had married drummer Al Spieldock, but she had never felt committed to him. Presented with the chance to travel with Shaw, she decided to leave her husband and join the band. In Shaw's band, her memories of her depressing childhood began to fade.

Then she went into Benny Goodman's band. Like many other singers and musicians, she found Goodman difficult to get along with; she quit before she went crazy from the strain. Furthermore, she was in love with the sound of Harry James's warm, sweetly blaring trumpet. She asked him for a job, telling him that she wanted arrangements built around her. She wanted to sing a whole song and even the introductory verse, if it was good. "I wanted to start with the band and finish with the band, not just sing a chorus in the middle of an instrumental as all the band singers were doing then," she said. Harry James hesitated, then agreed to do what she asked.[20]

She had learned phrasing from Billie Holiday and Artie Shaw. Benny Goodman's band had given her a greater feeling for swing, even though with him she had primarily done ballads such as "More Than You Know" and "The Man I Love." Then James began to feature his warm sound in tandem with Helen's solos, in arrangements that were tailor made for her. Helen was allowed to build up to exciting climaxes. The emotional, sentimental interpretations by the trumpeter and his singer made the band more famous than it had ever been. Helen won first place in *Metronome* and *Down Beat* magazine polls in 1942 and 1943.

Among her hits with James's band were "I Had the Craziest Dream," "I Don't Want to Walk Without You, Baby," "But Not For Me," "I've Heard That Song Before," and "He's My Guy." Because the band became more popular with Helen, a song that Sinatra had once recorded with the band was reissued. Originally it had sold sixteen thousand copies; now it sold nearly a million in 1942, on the Columbia label.

Helen fell in love with Harry James, a charming man liked by everyone. Unfortunately for Helen, he was unable to be faithful to one woman. She considered herself engaged to him, but he began to date other women. To further complicate her life, Al Spieldock wouldn't give her a divorce. He told her he didn't want her to marry Harry James. By 1943, when James—a slender man with bright blue eyes, sleek black hair, a crooked smile, and big ears that stuck out—took his band to Hollywood and appeared in movies, he no longer considered himself involved with Helen at all. The glamorous Hollywood star Betty Grable fascinated him instead. Her beautiful legs were insured for a million dollars each with Lloyd's of London. Grable was the number one pin-up girl with men in the armed services. Harry James married her in July 1943.

Heartbroken, Helen Forrest left James's band. When she opened on her own in New York, the critics wrote rave reviews. In Honolulu, she filled a club to overflowing. From $250 a week with James, she went to $2,500, she recalled, and sometimes more.[21] A club owner in the Midwest named his club for her—La Tête Rouge (French for "The Redhead"); she had dyed her hair red at that time. Later she bleached it very blonde and cut it short and feathery, a style that enhanced her dainty air.

Helen was married from the late 1950s to the early 1960s to a man who was in love with her career, not her. He wanted her to keep singing, while she wanted to stay home and take care of their son. By then, rock music had eclipsed her career in any case. She didn't find herself in demand again until supper clubs came back into fashion in the 1970s. Helen's autobiography, *I Had the Craziest Dream*, in which she confided she had always loved James, came out in 1981. James had left Grable for a younger showgirl, but by 1983 both James and Grable had died. Helen Forrest had outlived all those problems.

Ivie Anderson

Duke Ellington had begun leading his band in 1924 and played his own music with it from 1926 on. He treated the band, which was filled with wonderful soloists, as an instrument in itself, wresting from it a distinctive sound. He won a *Melody Maker* magazine poll in England in 1937, while white bands were winning the polls in America. Musicians regarded him as the greatest. He trailed in the polls in the United States because he had less exposure at home. His band couldn't play in all the hotels and theaters where white bands worked, and his music didn't get as much exposure on remote broadcasts. Furthermore, Duke didn't play the trendy, new tunes, only his own songs. Some of them, of course, became very popular. He created the song, "It Don't Mean a Thing If It Ain't Got That Swing," for which his band played "doo wah, doo wah, doo wah, doo wah." Everybody who knew anything about swing and big-band music knew that song. The lyrics became part of American legend and lore, culture and philosophy.

By 1936, he had found Ivie Anderson, a small, alert singer who could deliver his music with as much strength and command as his horn players did. She made a bright appearance with the band in a film called *Hit Parade* in 1937, singing the swinging ballad "I've Got to Be a Rug Cutter."

An orphan, Ivie had grown up in convents, where she was named Mary. She set out for New York in her midteens and became a Cotton Club chorus girl and second lead singer. She traveled around quite a bit to work and played in some South Side clubs in Chicago. Earl "Fatha" Hines hired her to play with his band. Then Ivie got the job with Duke.

She played in places ranging from rickety dives to glamorous hotels, with a bunch of "ruffians," as her special friend in the band, drummer Sonny Greer, called the band members.[22] Ivie had sharp little features, never wore much makeup, and always dressed in white to look angelic, stylish, and above it all. Actually she was full of life. She had many boyfriends and perhaps several husbands—later on, people could not

Ivie Anderson, shown here with Duke Ellington in 1934, was one of his best-loved band singers in the 1930s and 1940s. Onstage, she always dressed in white and achieved an angelic aura.

remember exactly how many. But she looked untouchable. She had learned to deliver lyrics—to unfurl them, taking her time with them, with a lot of vibrato—by listening to Ethel Waters at the Cotton Club. She had superb diction and knew exactly how and when to end her words. Her fashion sense, too, helped add class to the well-dressed Ellington band.

In performances, Sonny Greer catered to Ivie. He talked to her with his drums, and she answered him back. Audiences loved them. She was with the band on and off for about a dozen years. She sang such songs as "Life Is like a Cigarette," and Ellington's "Ebony Rhapsody" and "A Lonely Coed." Duke loved the way she delivered her own touching version of "Stormy Weather," even though he hadn't written it. One of her best-known songs with Duke's band was "I've Got It Bad and That Ain't Good."

But Ivie had a terrible health problem: asthma. Sometimes she suffered attacks just before she went onstage. When Ivie left the band for good in the late 1940s, Sonny Greer refused to have dialogues between his drums and other singers such as Joya Sherrill and Betty Roche. He knew they were good, but they just weren't his Ivie.

In Los Angeles, where she settled, she occasionally did singing dates. With Bobby Short (who later became the singer and pianist at New York's fashionable Cafe Carlyle), Ivie entertained prisoners in jails. She owned her own successful restaurant, Ivie's Chicken Shack, in the Central Avenue neighborhood of Los Angeles. She had left it in the care of friends, or boyfriends, throughout the 1940s, when she had traveled with Ellington. Musicians liked to go there. She married a man named Bart Neil when she retired from Duke's band officially in 1946. But Ivie died young, probably from asthma, in 1949.

Anita O'Day

Anita O'Day built such a solid career in the 1940s with her classy style that she could still attract large audiences to her concerts and fancy club dates in the 1990s. By then, she was in her mid-seventies and no longer had a good, supple voice; her pitch was uncertain. People applauded her, remembering how she had swung the old tune "Tea for Two" at a Newport Jazz Festival concert in 1958. Her performance defined the meaning of the word "swing."

That performance of Anita at the peak of her powers was captured on a film called *Jazz on a Summer Day*. Anita's rhythm was so driving that she sounded as if she was hovering over the stage. She became known as the finest authentic white jazz singer in the country. Later, she would write in her autobiography, *High Times, Hard Times*, that she had been high on heroin for the 1958 concert; she barely remembered it.[23] And she nearly died of her heroin addiction before she conquered it.

Anita began singing professionally as a teenager in the Depression era's dance contests; her mother had let her go out to make her own way. She thought her own greatest asset was her ability to sing. She had a different sound and a swinging style that seemed to take over her entire, slender body and emanate from her soul.

Strangely enough, she couldn't hold a note, and she had no vibrato. Instead of singing "aaaaaaaahhhhhhhh," she sang "ah-ah-ah-ah." It enhanced her swing. Eventually she found out that her idiosyncratic style was given to her accidentally by a doctor who had taken out her tonsils; during the operation, he had carelessly snipped off her uvula, the triangular piece of flesh at the entry to her throat.

Little is known about her earliest influences. She said that comedian Martha Raye impressed her; Raye was an excellent jazz singer early in her career in Chicago. Anita became very well known for her swinging duets on such tunes as "Let Me Off Uptown," with African-American trumpeter Roy Eldridge in Gene Krupa's band. But she left the band because of a strong personality conflict with Eldridge. She went to Stan Kenton's band. With her quick rhythmic sense, she could make the whole band swing.

Music, and not personal commitments, steered her through her turbulent life. And she was so influential as a jazz singer that both whites and African-Americans listened to her to learn their craft. Chris Connor and June Christy were both known as her disciples in jazz singing. When jazz critics and aficionados spoke about the best women jazz singers, they usually included Anita in the top four, and always in the top five, along with Billie, Ella, Sarah Vaughan, and often Carmen McRae.

In 1982, she performed in New York City for a week at the Blue Note. Even in her mid-sixties, she was tall, slender, and long-legged; she walked to the bandstand with posture so straight and proud that she looked regal. The past had not defeated her one iota. And what was her concept of jazz? A writer once asked her through drummer John Poole, her musical director and husband, who shouted the question into Anita's dressing room in a nightclub. She called back, "It's according to how good or bad the coffee is."[24]

It was a jive answer, but it carried with it an essential truth for Anita's approach to her craft. Jazz began with a feeling, and the feeling was elicited in her by her environment, which could include something as simple as the quality of the coffee. She was that suggestible. And as a jazz singer, she was a genius, able to use everything to inspire her.

These are just a few of the stories of the big-band jazz singers, who were drawn to jazz because of the expressiveness of the music and its infectious rhythms. Jazz gave them the freedom to improvise, to embellish melodies, and to assert their individuality.

After the big-band era ended in the late 1940s, it was almost impossible for a singer to dream of getting experience and exposure with a band. Among the few exceptions were Al Hibbler with Duke Ellington and Joe Williams with Count Basie in the 1950s. Their spectacular voices, supported by the artistry of the bands, allowed them to become famous during a time known as the "Golden Age of Singers," when singers usually worked on their own.

The Jazz Singing Tree

This outline focuses on the pivotal jazz singers throughout the twentieth century. Some were the best singers of their era and set standards for all singers to come. Others were innovators in the art of jazz singing. Some were both wonderful singers and innovators. Many had very long careers.

From the 1890s to the 1920s

Church singing was adapted to secular, worldly subjects by the blues singers. Two types of blues singers developed, country and city (or urban). Among the best-known blues singers, whose sophisticated, urban style led to the development of jazz singing, was *Bessie Smith.* Extremely popular in African-American communities, she had such a powerful voice that, even without a microphone, she could make herself heard in the top balconies of theaters. Discovered by a great talent scout and record producer, John Hammond, she recorded for Columbia Records and became a darling of society people in the Jazz Age of the 1920s. Her career lasted until the 1930s.

Bessie Smith

From the 1920s

Ethel Waters, a bluesy pop singer from Philadelphia, traveled around the country, performing in theaters and clubs, until she settled in New York and established herself in Harlem clubs. By 1925, in her late twenties, she had a hit recording of "Dinah." She could spellbind an audience by the way she told her songs with her phrasing, intonation, and beautiful soprano voice. Other singers studied her style. Among her best-known admirers in her generation was vaudevillian *Sophie Tucker,* a singer and comedienne. Ethel influenced many singers, male and female, in the 1930s and 1940s.

Regarded as the founder of modern jazz for the way he played his trumpet,

Louis Armstrong

Louis Armstrong was also admired for his singing. His vocal style was an extension of his trumpet playing. In 1928, leading his own group in a recording studio, he sang "West End Blues," a whimsical scat song (that is, a song without words), which many experts called the first definitive jazz song. Other budding singers, who heard Armstrong sing on records and in person, imbibed his influence. He improvised by singing notes that the chords of the written songs suggested; he glided or slid from note to note for a more plaintive, affecting musicality; with uniquely creative phrasing, he developed his stories.

In his native New Orleans, Armstrong had listened to Cajun scat singers, early blues and pop singers, and many other stylists. He heard them in the streets, joints, and theaters. He may even have heard Ethel Waters, who was a few years older than he. Waters toured the country before Armstrong migrated north to Chicago.

Mildred Bailey, influenced by Bessie Smith's recordings, became a very popular singer and recording artist with the Paul Whiteman big band in the 1920s. One of her great admirers was *Lee Wiley,* a younger singer who became popular in the 1930s and 1940s. Both of these white singers had a great influence on the white big-band singers from about 1934 to 1947.

Bing Crosby also got a chance to perform with Paul Whiteman in the 1920s before becoming a star in the 1930s. One of his first role models was Al Jolson, a white vaudevillian who paid attention to the early blues

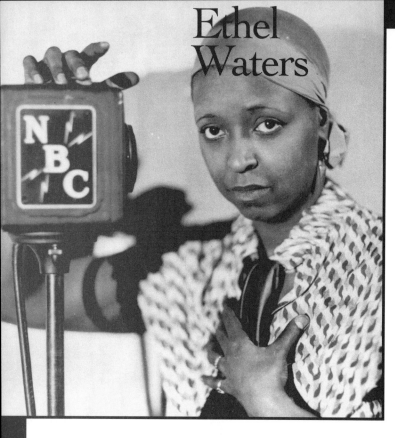

Ethel Waters

singers and became one of the most popular entertainers in the country. Then Crosby discovered Louis Armstrong. When Crosby became a movie star, he took Armstrong with him.

Crosby, an extremely popular singer whose career spanned about fifty years, influenced many young baritones, including **Perry Como, Vic Damone,** and **Dick Haymes.** Their careers developed in the big-band era and continued strong in the 1950s. Crosby also influenced the great dancer **Fred Astaire,** who also sang in movies. **Rosemary Clooney,** a big-band singer with Tony Pastor in the 1940s, had a nationwide hit with the tune "Come On-a My House" in 1950; she called Crosby an important role model for her song stylings.

Cab Calloway, with his robust tenor voice, began leading his own band in the 1920s. He established himself as a major singing star in the 1930s. He was called the "hi-de-ho man" for his unique scat style.

From the 1930s

Some people have called **Billie Holiday** the most authentic female jazz singer in history. Her laid-back, plaintive sound, her brilliant timing, and her improvisational ideas have won her extremely devoted fans. She listened to Louis Armstrong and Bessie Smith for inspiration, became a recording artist beginning in 1933 in small groups in New York, went on the road with the Count Basie and Artie Shaw big bands in the late 1930s, and by 1939 established herself as a star in New York's first integrated club, Café Society Downtown. Nearly every singer after her — white, African-American, or Asian — listened to Billie Holiday for instruction and inspiration. During her lifetime, because of her eccentric sound and scandalous lifestyle, she never achieved the fame or riches of several other singers. But after her death in 1959, as her recordings were reissued and played constantly, she became an American legend.

Billie Holiday

Ella Fitzgerald began singing with Chick Webb's big band in the 1930s and had a hit recording, "A Tisket, A Tasket." After Webb died, Fitzgerald inherited the band. Then the musicians were drafted to fight in World War II. She recorded for Decca for many years. In the 1950s, a great jazz entrepreneur, Norman Granz, became her manager and guided her career to make her the most commercially successful singer in jazz history. She sang songbooks of the nation's greatest popular music composers. Artistically, too, she was exceptional, with a magical control of rhythm. Consistently she won first

Cab Calloway

place in the jazz polls over other fine singers, including Billie Holiday and Sarah Vaughan. She has always been a standard against which other singers measure themselves.

Another important band singer was *Anita O'Day,* who began singing as a teenager in the 1930s, played with drummer Gene Krupa's band, and then with Stan Kenton's very popular and adventurous big band. O'Day, who is white, is often regarded as one of the most influential female jazz singers, along with Billie Holiday, Ella Fitzgerald, and Sarah Vaughan. Swinging the song "Tea for Two" at the Newport Jazz Festival in 1958, she was caught on film for the popular documentary *Jazz on a Summer's Day* and became a symbol of jazz. She cited Martha Raye, known primarily as a comedienne, as the singer from whom she learned the most about jazz singing. (In the early days of her career, Raye sang jazz in Chicago, performing with such stars as pianist Earl "Fatha" Hines.)

Mel Tormé, a child singing star in his native Chicago in the 1930s, went to Hollywood, where he was featured in movies. Angelic looking, with a soft, intimate sound that was characteristic of traditional jazz, he was called the "Velvet Fog." As the years passed, his excellence became obvious to audiences, musicians, and critics. His career as a singer, arranger, composer, and bandleader has continued into the 1990s.

Ella Fitzgerald

Anita
O'Day

African-American beauty *Lena Horne,* who appeared at the Cotton Club in Harlem in the 1930s, sang with both white and African-American big bands. She starred in films and kept developing her artistry, until she became a first-class jazz singer. As much as Billie Holiday lagged behind the beat, Lena sometimes sped up and sang ahead of it with exciting results.

Sarah Vaughan had the most beautiful and affecting voice in jazz. Some people cried when they heard her sing "Summertime," "Send in the Clowns," "The Lord's Prayer," and other staples of her repertoire. She began her illustrious career as a band singer with Earl "Fatha" Hines in 1943. Her ability to sing complicated music made her a darling of the young beboppers in the 1940s. She developed into the greatest diva in jazz, influencing every singer of her generation and thereafter. In 1982, she won a Grammy for an album of George Gershwin's music done in 1981 with symphony orchestra conductor Michael Tilson Thomas.

Also in the 1930s and 1940s, many big-band singers developed their talents. When the big-band era ended, they went on to become stars

From the 1940s

on their own. The most important has been *Frank Sinatra.* He was a skinny kid from Hoboken, New Jersey, who began singing with Harry James's band. He then switched to the more established bandleader Tommy Dorsey, a trombonist. From Dorsey, Sinatra learned phrasing. Sinatra's career went into an eclipse for awhile, because of his tumultuous personal life and legendary temper, but he made a comeback by winning an Academy Award for the movie *From Here to Eternity* in 1953. He subsequently reestablished his eminence as a singer and became the single greatest superstar in jazz- and pop-singing history. Other singers worship his phrasing and storytelling abilities, which are among the most important elements of his brash and romantic style.

Sarah Vaughan

Peggy Lee established herself in 1941 as Benny Goodman's band singer. She went on to have major hits as a singer and songwriter on her own and maintained her stardom into the 1990s. *Jimmy Rushing*, a blues singer with Count Basie in the 1930s and 1940s, and *Ivie Anderson,* Duke Ellington's bandsinger in the 1940s, did their best-known work with their bands.

Carmen McRae, who spent fifteen years painstakingly establishing her career, became famous for her ability to tell a story within a song. She had

From the 1950s

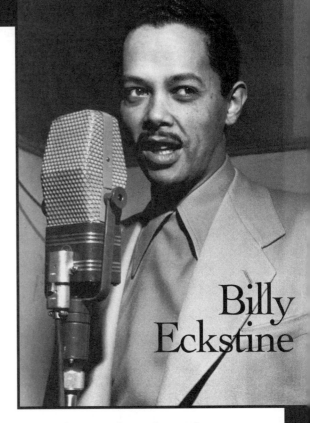

Billy Eckstine

a magical way of communicating with an audience. Young singers took lessons from her dramatic style and adventurous harmonic sense. Many consider her as authentic as Billie Holiday and as influential for the art of jazz singing as Ella Fitzgerald and Sarah Vaughan. *Billy Eckstine,* who attracted crowds to Earl Hines's band in the late 1930s and 1940s, had a big hit with the blues song "Jelly Jelly." He went out on his own as a bebop bandleader. By 1950, when he had begun to emphasize his electrifying vibrato and sing romantic ballads such as "I Apologize" on the Columbia label, he became a major star and matinee idol. An extremely handsome African-American, he attracted female fans of all races. They chased him constantly. Admirers of his success, several other African-American baritones tried to follow in Eckstine's footsteps. Some succeeded, to an extent, such as *Al Hibbler* and *Arthur Prysock*.

An especially fine singer, *Johnny Hartman,* had less commercial suc-

Peggy Lee

cess, possibly because of his shy style in live performances. But on recordings he is a master and at least an equal to Eckstine.

Tony Bennett, who learned from jazz instrumentalists, particularly the horn players, was grateful to Billy Eckstine for encouragement. Bennett became a recording star in the 1950s with such songs as "I Left My Heart in San Francisco." His career went into eclipse with the advent of the reign of rock and roll in the 1960s. But during the renaissance of jazz's commercial appeal in the 1980s and 1990s, Bennett ascended to stardom again. He attributes his popularity to his ability to pick wonderful songs and perform with the best jazz and jazz-influenced musicians, but he also has an exciting, warm baritone and technical mastery of his art.

Joe Williams, who began as a ballad singer based in Chicago, also

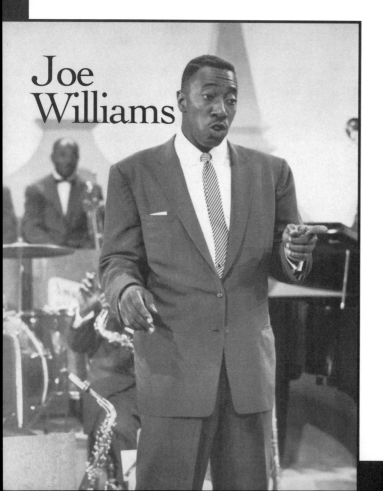

Joe
Williams

liked to sing some blues. He became famous as a very sophisticated urban blues singer with Count Basie's band beginning in 1954. Six years later, Williams began leading his own groups, and he established his mastery of interpreting ballads and all types of popular songs. More than any other African-American jazz singer except for Eckstine and Nat King Cole, Williams exerted a special influence over aspiring singers who followed him. In the 1990s, his mere appearance onstage often prompts a standing ovation.

Nat King Cole, first a jazz pianist, formed the King Cole Trio with a bassist and guitarist in Los Angeles in 1937. He also sang with the trio. They struggled until 1943, when they began having hits. By the end of the 1940s, Cole rarely played piano. Instead, he stood up to sing at a microphone. He drew upon his jazz background for his rhythms and improvisations, though he became best known, in the 1950s, as a popular singer. He had a small note range, but his velvety voice and intimate style put his stories across well to adoring fans. His singing hits included "The Christmas Song,"

Nat "King" Cole

"Nature Boy," "Mona Lisa," and "Rambling Rose." In 1958, he became the first African-American entertainer to have a nationwide television show. Long after his death in 1965, his enduring fame through recordings helped his very talented daughter Natalie become a star.

Chris Connor and **June Christy** took their inspiration from Anita O'Day and, like her, sang with Stan Kenton's band. Both singers are among the most important in the tradition.

Dinah Washington, who started out singing gospel music, developed as a powerful blues, pop, and jazz singer. She had a major influence on popular singers of all those styles from the 1950s on, including **Dakota Stanton, Nancy Wilson, Aretha Franklin,** and **Bette Midler.**

Other singers with big bands, among them **Doris Day** and **Betty Hutton,** parlayed their excellent voices, jazz-influenced styles, and charming personalities into major movie careers in Hollywood.

Instead of following the path of popular singers to fame and fortune, some vocalists became deeply involved in the efforts and explorations of jazz instrumentalists. The singing group Lambert, Hendricks, and Ross (**Dave Lambert, Jon Hendricks,** and **Annie Ross**) put words to horn solos of important swing-era bands, particularly Count Basie's, and they sang at breakneck speed. Eddie Jefferson wrote lyrics for the great improvised bebop horn

From the late 1950s into the 1970s

solos. James Moody's tune "Moody's Mood for Love," for example, derived from the chords of the pop standard "I'm in the Mood for Love."

These singers heralded the arrival of ever more adventurous jazz singers, who

Dinah Washington

played increasingly experimental music. Unfortunately, audiences were looking for a simpler, more entertaining, and easily accessible music. The times had changed and were continuing to change. In the turbulent society of the United States in the 1960s, people wanted the elemental beat of rock. Jazz became a specialized art music.

Rock dominated the pop-music world in the 1960s. By the end of the decade, rhythm and blues, which shared with jazz its roots in African-American gospel and blues music, became extremely popular. Other types of music, too—folk, and country and western, for example—captured the fancy of the public. Some jazz musicians, such as saxophonist Stan Getz, who loved pretty melodies, combined jazz with Brazilian music. They brought this hybrid into the American mainstream. Singer *Astrud Gilberto* had hits in the 1960s with her seductive, soft Brazilian sound.

A popular trumpeter, *Chet Baker,* became known for his cool style of playing and singing in the 1950s. He was also known for his scan-

Lambert, Hendricks, and Ross

dalous heroin habit, and he struggled to maintain a career as a first-rate musician. He spent most of his time in Europe, where audiences still loved jazz. He had a uniquely mesmerizing, soft tenor voice. His style seemed effortless and inimitable.

Helen Merrill, who loved to sing the flatted fifths that are emblematic of the bebop style, made a highly praised album in the mid-1950s. But work for a jazz singer became scarce. By the early 1960s, she went to live and work in Europe, where she could support herself and her son. Other excellent contemporary singers with their roots in traditional jazz and bebop—*Carol Sloane, Mark Murphy, Jackie Paris,* and *Anne Marie Moss* among them—also had difficulty establishing commercially viable careers in the 1960s. *Geri Southern* became a popular recording artist and singer/pianist. She provided intermission entertainment at the club Birdland. She went to Hollywood and became a music teacher and composer.

People who had established themselves before the reign of rock usually were able to maintain viable careers. Sarah Vaughan, for one, worked in Las Vegas clubs, hotels, jazz festivals, and theaters, and she dreamed of becoming a concert artist. She began realizing her goal in the 1970s, when she first collaborated with Michael Tilson Thomas in a concert.

The new popularity of instrumental jazz, which resurfaced as rock concerts became dangerous and lost some of their appeal, revitalized the careers of the older singers. Young instrumentalists began to get their chances to record and perform with important groups in first-rate clubs and concert halls.

1980s

Young singers still found it difficult to get work. Among the few who succeeded are the multitalented singers *Al Jarreau* and *Bobby McFerrin.* Jarreau had his roots deep in the jazz mainstream. He also loved to sing with electronic instruments and explore music from other cultures. McFerrin, who had studied music and performance in college, utilized eclectic sources for inspiration. In performance, he reproduces nature sounds and drums on his chest as if it were a hollow gourd. He often gives solo concerts, accompanying himself with myriad musical sounds produced miraculously and solely by his mouth and body. *Cassandra Wilson* attracted attention with her eccentric improvisations based on such songs as "Blue Skies" and "Polka Dots and Moonbeams." An experimentalist, she maintained public interest throughout her career.

Wilson's main inspiration was *Betty Carter,* the only experimental singer who could fill a club or a concert hall for her unusual harmonic adventures. She performed original songs and eccentric interpretations of popular standards. Her style was

Betty Carter

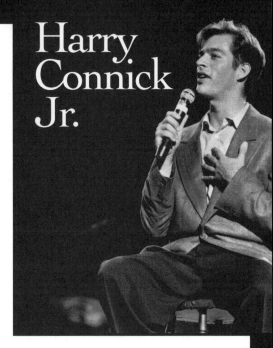

iconoclastic; she pulled apart the old songs and made them into something new.

Betty had begun working with Lionel Hampton in the 1940s. He called her "Betty Bebop," a nickname she disliked at the time. Later she felt grateful to him for forcing her to become adventurous. She is mentioned so late in this "tree" because she did not become accepted—that is, a well-known, highly praised, commercially viable jazz singer—until audiences caught up with her concept in the 1980s.

But other fine experimental singers, despite praise from critics, had less luck and weathered hard times. *Jay Clayton* decided to take a job teaching vocal jazz and improvisation in a college in Washington state in the 1980s. *Janet Lawson*, who has a beautiful soprano voice and a Grammy nomination for an album of experimental vocal jazz, left New York for a home in the countryside.

As the older singers, who had dominated the art, began to retire or die, jazz fans and record producers became increasingly worried about the

1990s

dearth of young singers to carry on the tradition. Young singers began to have an easier time getting recording contracts and gigs in clubs and concert halls. To some audiences, the young singers seemed to materialize magically. Actually, many of them had been waiting in the wings for years, earning rave reviews whenever they could find a few jobs.

Among the best to step into the shoes of the masters were *Judy Niemack, Vanessa Rubin, Nnenna Freelon, Jeanie Bryson* (who is Dizzy Gillespie's daughter), *Carla White, Dee Dee Bridgewater* (a star who lives in Paris), *Harry Connick Jr.* (a pianist and Sinatra-in-training), guitarist/singer *John Pizzarelli Jr.* (a devotee of Nat King Cole), *Diana Krall, Diane Reeves, Kurt Elling* (bebop heir and experimentalist), *Giacomo Gates* (a worshipper of Eddie Jefferson), *Susannah Mc Corkle,* who learned to sing by listening to Billie Holiday records, and classically-trained *Weslia Whitfield.* These and many other artists all worked to remain true to certain facets of the tradition of jazz.

Following in the footsteps of Joe Williams and Billy Eckstine is *Kevin Mahogany,* a strapping, impressive-looking man well over six feet tall. He spent ten years working in his native Kansas City before he got a recording contract with Enja and acquired a wide audience in the 1990s. He thrilled jazz fans who had thought they would never again hear a young man singing as well as the old masters had done.

Kevin Mahogany

Chapter Six **The Bebop Influence**

A revolution in jazz began at the height of the big-band era's popularity. Every singer and musician would be affected by the embellishments and sophistications of the new jazz style called bebop. The style put special demands on jazz singers and expanded their musical horizons. After the development of bebop, jazz singers would follow widely divergent paths. Some would incorporate bebop accents into their popular jazz styles. Others used bebop as a springboard to get into more experimental singing. Some prominent singers moved back and forth between commercial and experimental music.

The experimenters in this movement stressed odd harmonies, unusual tempos, and abstract melodies, and they explored rhythms and harmonies popular in foreign cultures. They also explored ancient and exotic ways of organizing music—by themes or modes, for example, instead of scales.

Swingers and Crooners

They brought into their music all kinds of unusual sounds from their environment. Bebop opened doors to new horizons for jazz singers and instrumentalists.

In the early 1940s, bebop's inventors congregated in pianist Earl "Fatha" Hines's band. Hines led one of the best, most popular African-American dance bands during the swing era. Budd Johnson, a tenor saxophonist in the band, brought Hines to a club to hear a fine young baritone with a high, thrilling voice and straightforward style. Hines hired the singer Billy Eckstine, who was one of the most handsome men in the country—penetrating eyes, even features, a mustache, perfect teeth, and a rakish smile that radiated sex appeal. Billy gained confidence and stagecraft by watching Hines. The band's horn players also helped Billy, whom they nicknamed "B," to build technique. Eager to understand all he could about music, B started playing trumpet, valve trombone, and guitar. Almost by accident he and the band had a great success in the early 1940s with a blues song called "Jelly Jelly."

In a recording studio, they needed one more song to round out a date. The man in the recording session asked them if they had a blues tune. "Earl Hines and the band got this little head arrangement [music not written down] of a twelve-bar blues," B recalled. "Then all we had to do was write the lyrics. So I went outside and wrote them. I don't know what inspired me. Nothing that was going on in my personal life."[1]

Eckstine sang his song about trying to call his girlfriend on the phone and being filled with love and desire for her. He called his passion "jelly." That was what had killed so many people, including his father, he lamented. "Jelly Jelly" had done it.

Traveling constantly in their popular band, Eckstine and Johnson, who became close friends, listened to young instrumentalists experimenting with the chords of written songs at Minton's Playhouse in Harlem. They embellished the songs in many ways, complicating the harmonies and the rhythms. From those elements, their improvisations became so elaborate that they took on a life of their own. The young progressives

100

played entirely new lines over the written chords, and they changed the chords, too, developing new harmonies.

These musicians began composing totally new songs. The style in which they played was more driving and aggressive, played at much faster, complex, intense, and choppy tempos than the swing era's dance-band music. One journalist thought a drummer's choppy rhythm sounded like the word "bebop." He may have been the one who dubbed the entire style "bebop." Other journalists heard trumpeter Dizzy Gillespie and the other revolutionaries calling out scat words that sounded like rebop and bebop to signal each other what tune they were going to play. The word "bebop" caught on with the public. Although bebop had a more intro-spective, intellectual, and rebellious attitude than swing, B and Budd convinced Earl Hines to hire a few of the new cats playing that interest-ing new music.

Cab Calloway hadn't liked it. He accused Dizzy of playing what he called Chinese music. "Pops" Armstrong hadn't liked much bebop, either. But Hines knew that young people wanted to hear a taste of that new sound, with all its squeaks, squeals, awesome runs and interval leaps, and odd meters. So he hired its two primary inventors, Dizzy and alto saxo-phonist Charlie "Bird" Parker. They settled into the band for a while.

In 1942, a gawky, skinny girl named Sarah Vaughan borrowed money from her high school friends and took two trains from Newark, New Jersey, to get to the Apollo Theater for the Wednesday night ama-teur contest. She had played piano to accompany a singer there once before. Now she was going to try her luck as a singer herself. She chose "Body and Soul," a ballad which both tenor saxophonist Coleman Hawkins and Billie Holiday had recorded to great praise.

Sarah was terrified about performing at the Apollo. Audiences there hooted at performers they didn't like. Her dress was no better than a house dress. Her hair was a mess. The master of ceremonies worried about her, because she looked so small. But she sang from her heart, and she was able to improvise on the chords and jump octaves as easily as a kitten plays with a ball of yarn. Her voice was so beautiful that the audience screamed approval. She won first prize, ten dollars, and a week's engagement at the Apollo.[2]

Ella Fitzgerald, who was headliner at the theater that week, kept Sarah from signing contracts with hustlers pretending to be agents. B had gone to hear Ella; he fell in love with Sarah's singing and told Hines about her. Listening to Sarah, Hines turned to a friend and said, "Is that girl singing, or am I drunk or what?"[3] In April 1943, Sarah made her debut with Hines's band at the Apollo.

Sarah Vaughan had studied piano, played organ, and sung in a Baptist church in Newark. She had also dropped out of high school to sing and play in Newark's clubs. She was always hanging around musicians and listening to music live, on records, and on the radio. That was how she developed her style, learned techniques, and gained experience. The new music played by Bird and Dizzy in Hines's band enthralled her. "She didn't want to know about nothing but Bird's music," Dizzy noted.[4]

Sarah was so gifted that she could sing whatever the musicians played. Hines bought her a pretty white gown with a peplum, because she had no stage clothes. After the dress got a hole from a cigarette burn in the back, she never turned around onstage. She didn't know how to dress or groom herself, but from her experiences with musicians in nightclubs in Newark, she knew exactly how to get along with the cats in the band. It was easy for her to join in when they gambled, played pranks, went to movies, and drank in clubs of all sorts.

She also knew how to unfurl her remarkable voice slowly and use the shimmering little ripples of her vibrato for dramatic purposes. The richness of her timbre led people to describe her sound as smoky. She could wave the word "me" up and down in the song "Once in a While," imbuing it with the characteristic intimacy and softness of jazz. Another big-band singer might belt the song, but not Sarah. She could luxuriate in the drawn-out words "once," "I," "you," "two," and "apart," and make them so lush that, with those words alone, she communicated a message of romance. She could rise to a high note no one else could think of hitting, and, with her unique vocal quality, hold the beautiful note, change keys, and finish a song on a purer, even higher note. A less creative singer would look to the written music for guidance. Sarah could build from a mature-sounding contralto to a haunting, glowing coloratura soprano within one song.

Sarah's style was influenced by Billy Eckstine's tastes, too. One of B's great strengths was the unhurried way he drew out ballads with his rich baritone. As he grew older, his voice deepened. He sang with increasing vibrato. He knew exactly which types of songs to sing and which to reject. When Billy and Sarah sang romantic duets together in Hines's band, their sound was intoxicating.

Sarah looked up to B, who was ten years older than she, as a suave, romantic, independent man. Although she was toughened from hanging out in jazz clubs, she could still be sweet and girlish; when B teased her because she was naive about good grooming or anything else, she giggled.

Singing with Hines, B became very popular; eventually, he wanted to lead his own band. Dizzy kept urging him on. B dreamed of featuring the new music, and Dizzy wanted to play it all the time, not just once in a while as he did in the Hines band. Finally B decided to start a band with the backing of a prominent management firm. He hired Dizzy as musical director. Bird came in, too. Sarah lingered with the Hines band for a while, but then she also joined B.

Some people thought Sarah was so good that she drew attention away from B. For whatever reason, she left his band in 1944. With lessons learned from him about stagecraft, phrasing, and choice of songs, she sang with little groups on the road and in 52nd Street clubs. Eckstine told other singers: "Go to hear Sarah Vaughan. It will do your heart good." Sarah's first recording date, done with Dizzy and Bird on New Year's Eve of 1944, led to her own recording contract with a small company, Musicraft.

She found a job as a singer with the house band at Cafe Society Downtown. One night, John Hammond, who had recorded Bessie Smith and discovered Billie Holiday, went to hear the show there. But

Hammond was still totally devoted to the blues and swing-era artists at that time, and he just read a newspaper ringside while Sarah sang. She became scared to death that she might have a bleak future.[5]

But her voice completely seduced a young trumpet player, George Treadwell, who was playing at the club. After work, he and Sarah, who had already earned the nickname "Sassy," because she sometimes had that attitude, took a subway to 52nd Street. They shared their dreams of becoming famous, she as a singer, he as an artist's manager. "They fell in love on the A train," said Johnnie Garry, a friend who worked as a stage-hand at Cafe Society.[6]

George and Sarah married. He took charge of her career; he had her teeth capped to hide a gap between her front teeth; he threw away her high-piled wig and got her hair styled. His mother sewed a wardrobe for Sarah. George said he had used his eight thousand dollars in savings to launch Sarah. The truth was he had just about enough money for a wedding license, but he did know how to manage Sarah's career. He taught her how to use makeup and how to move onstage. Their strengths blended magically. Under his guidance, Sarah went from Musicraft to Columbia. Her club bookings became bigger and better. Dave Garroway, a famous radio personality on the NBC station in Chicago, fell in love with her voice and played her records all the time on his show. He even asked Sarah to sing "Tenderly" on the telephone to his wife.

Some of Sarah's early records became popular. Others were acclaimed as works of art. Among the best were "I Cover the Waterfront" and "The Lord's Prayer." *Time* magazine took notice. But her elaborate style caused controversy. An argument broke out between a Chicago newspaper critic, who wrote that she was a terrible singer and that jazz was dead, and a *Down Beat* critic who rushed to defend Sarah's great voice and modern style. Sarah went on to do a record that sold a million copies, "Broken Hearted Melody"; it was a pop tune, unlike her usual, complicated jazz songs. No matter what she sang, though, she did it with a creamy-smooth voice and adventurous harmonic sensibilities. She became a star.

As she became popular, her marriage to Treadwell failed. They fought all the time because he told her what to do and whom to be friendly with. He wanted her to talk to rich, influential people. She was most comfortable talking in slang with her old friends from Newark. He became jealous when men flirted with her in clubs. Sarah did as she pleased. Sometimes she provoked fights on purpose to counteract Treadwell's bossiness. Furthermore, she was a new star, with money and attention for the first time in her life. She wanted to try her wings and see how high she could fly. A hairdresser who traveled with Sarah thought that she and George loved each other but that they were too young and immature.

Sarah went on to marry and have affairs with other men. They always became involved in her management, even if they had no experience. Her demanding career overshadowed her relationships. And the career had its ups and downs at times, because its management wasn't good enough. Her moodiness became notorious. She loved to have a good time and stay up three days and nights at a time. She hung out, listened to music, snorted cocaine, and cooked and ate enormous meals that put far too much weight on her. She shopped, watched TV, read comic books, and played golf—whatever suited her fancy on the spur of the moment.

To clear her throat, she would suck on a lemon slice with sugar on it, a trick used by many singers. Otherwise she did nothing to protect her voice. Roy Haynes, who played drums in her group for years, noticed that she could spend a weekend partying continuously and then show up at a recording studio on Monday morning with her voice as clear as a bell. "The bitch is a genius," he told a friend.[7]

Occasionally she and B crossed paths. Eckstine had broken up his bebop band in 1947 and became one of the most popular ballad singers in the country. Love songs at medium-slow tempos were his strongest material. Women of all races, and teenagers, too, mobbed stage doors where he worked. Sarah always loved him. Simply the way she looked at him made her friends realize how much she respected him.

Swingers and Crooners

B's great hits done in the 1950s — "I Apologize," "I Surrender, Dear," and "My Foolish Heart" — kept him popular with audiences for the rest of his life. In 1957, he and Sarah recorded duets. The most popular was "Passing Strangers," but others were just as fine a blending of their voices and styles. At the end of the song "Isn't It a Lovely Day?" B said: "Wow, what a crazy day, Sass," and she responded by giggling. On "Easter Parade," B sang about seeing their pictures in the "rotogravure," enunciating that word so elegantly that it seemed like the greatest place in the world to be seen. His strong voice, with a thrilling vibrato that seemed to come straight from his heart, began to falter in the 1970s. People kept going to hear him for sentimental reasons.

Sarah's powers never diminished. Even when jazz lost its commercial appeal in the 1960s and rock reigned in the pop music world, she always found work in pretty cocktail lounges and gambling casinos in Las Vegas. Critics always praised her. In the 1970s, a classical orchestra conductor, Michael Tilson Thomas, called her to do a concert of Gershwin songs with him and a symphony orchestra in Los Angeles. It was a great success commercially and artistically. After that, Sarah added concert halls to her itinerary of clubs, jazz concerts, and jazz festivals.

In 1981, she made an all-Gershwin recording with Michael Tilson Thomas on the Columbia label. A friend went to see Sarah in a concert at Lincoln Center, the great performing arts center in New York. Backstage, she led him by the hand to a ladies' room, shut the door, and asked him how he liked the Gershwin record. He said, "I love it. How do you like it?" She whooped and shouted, "I love it!" She thought it was the best thing she had ever done.

The album won a Grammy — her first. In the 1980s, jazz became popular again, and Sarah's career became more illustrious than ever. Her voice deepened and became richer with age. She could make people cry when she sang her trademark songs "Misty," "Send in the Clowns," and "Summertime."

106

Then her musicians noticed she had trouble catching her breath on long walks through airports. In 1990, at age sixty-six, she began to lose the use of her left arm. Medical tests revealed that she had lung cancer. She went to her splendid house in Hidden Hills, California, and underwent treatments. They didn't work. Her friend Robert Richards visited her; they took a drive and talked about her life, not her illness. Over the years, she had lost a great deal of money to three husbands and many boyfriends. Her second husband had left her in a quarter of a million dollars of debt. She had also given money away to friends in need—even to Billy Eckstine, who ended up with serious financial problems. She told Richards she wished she could run through all her money again. "And this time I'd like to spend all the money myself," she said.[8]

Many other friends visited her and called her. They said she could still sing until the last few days of her life. She died on April 4, 1990. A couple of years later, Billy Eckstine died in Pittsburgh, his hometown, where his niece took care of him after he suffered a stroke and couldn't perform anymore.

Some other singers based their entire careers on the bebop style. One was Jackie Paris, who first caught the attention of the public in the 1940s on 52nd Street. Eddie Jefferson was the first singer to write lyrics for the new bebop songs. His lyrics for "Moody's Mood for Love," written for James Moody's saxophone improvisation based on the tune "I'm in the Mood for Love," became an enduring popular song in its own right. Thelonious Monk's moody "Round Midnight" became doubly famous when a writer added lyrics about how the burden of lost love became unbearable 'round midnight.

Many singers recorded arresting songs with Dizzy Gillespie's group, among them Babs Gonzalez and Joe Carroll. Dizzy loved the scat lyrics they put to his music. A singer named King Pleasure wrote lyrics for "Lester Leaps In." It became "Jumping with My Boy Sid in the City," the theme song for a radio show hosted by a New York jazz disc jockey called "Symphony Sid."

Swingers and Crooners

Several very stylish bebop singing groups became well known. First came Lambert, Hendricks, and Ross, two men and a woman, who put words to solos played by legendary swing-era and bebop horn players. Lambert, Hendricks, and Ross sang, in true bebop style, at breakneck speed.

Many years later, long after the group had broken up, Jon Hendricks was still performing in the same style with members of his own family and with young singers he hired. One of these singers in the early 1980s was Bobby McFerrin, who later struck out on his own and became a Grammy-winning superstar with pop songs such as "Don't Worry, Be Happy" and musical innovations of all sorts.

Lambert, Hendricks, and Ross (with Dave Lambert and Annie Ross) influenced many young singers. Mark Murphy, for one, who also regarded Eddie Jefferson as a primary influence, followed Hendricks around and studied his technique. Murphy went to live in Paris during the reign of rock. Al Jarreau, who emerged as a jazz-pop star in the 1980s, considered Hendricks a chief influence. Obvious disciples of Lambert, Hendricks, and Ross were two other groups, the Manhattan Transfer and the New Hi-Los. Less obviously, but nevertheless a descendant of the beboppers, was the pop-gospel group Take Five, which became prominent in the late 1980s.

"I know people who sing better than we do," Jon Hendricks once said about his groups. "But we'll swing all of them into bad health. I don't care if my voice is not as clear as a bell. I'm more interested in emotion than notes. If the feeling is groovy, I'll take that over the right notes. Jazz is feeling and emotion. The right notes are for the classical field. Guys may be more technically proficient than Louis Armstrong. But he could make you cry. That was his greatness."[9]

Chapter Seven **Singers on Their Own**

Some singers, who had missed out on stardom during the big-band era, experienced some real loneliness on their path to fame and fortune. But they made it.

Joe Williams

Singer Joe Williams, born in Cordele, Georgia, on December 12, 1918, and raised in Chicago, began singing at age sixteen in clubs on Chicago's South Side. Everyone knew he could sing beautifully, but he wasn't getting any big breaks. When times were very tough, he worked all day as a door-to-door cosmetics salesman for the Fuller Brush Company, and he spent his nights in clubs, singing for relatively little money. Performing

109

with bands that had excellent reputations, he even worked briefly with Count Basie for fifty dollars a week in a Chicago club in the early 1940s. But Joe's career wasn't stable.

In his early thirties, Joe became very depressed by his struggles and needed psychiatric care.[1] Later he would make that part of his life public, to offer hope and inspiration to others. But he always knew he was a very good singer. Even when he thought he might never get ahead, he decided to keep singing. That made him happy. When he wasn't working, he went into a park and sang to the birds for practice.

At last, when Joe was thirty-seven years old, Count Basie invited him to join the band. Basie needed someone with a forceful, beautiful baritone to sing the blues. During World War II, Basie hadn't been able to support a big band and a singer. In the 1950s, people fell in love with his appealing, blues-based, brassy sound all over again. They showed up to listen, not to dance. Basie often starred in Birdland, New York's most famous jazz club. Joe had made a name for himself primarily as a ballad singer. His voice was smooth, his diction very clear. Most blues singers had strong regional accents. But Joe understood the authentic blues spirit; he sang a very exciting version of "Every Day," about always having the blues.

When Joe sang with Basie's band, he electrified audiences with his voice and vitality. He could soar over Basie's brass section. He could dive through it. He called out to instruments and answered them in his supple voice. He danced an octave away from the melody and back. His voice could become dramatic and seductive with vibrato, or clear and innocent as a blue sky on a sunny morning. He could do anything the horn players could do. Seemingly overnight, he became a star, and Basie's band went on to greater international fame than it had ever enjoyed before.

Joe stayed with Basie, singing mostly blues songs, with authority and ease, from Christmas Day of 1954 until 1960. Later on, when they worked together for special engagements, Basie called Joe "my number one son."[2] By then Joe had distinguished himself as a leader of his own group, singing ballads, blues, and any other type of song that appealed to him—even country and western. He performed at Carnegie Hall, Royal Albert Hall in London, and awards ceremonies at the Kennedy Center in Washington, D.C. People have always associated Joe with Basie, but Joe has spent more than thirty-five years on his own.

Joe learned from Nat "King" Cole's easy-mannered delivery and Frank Sinatra's style on ballads with Tommy Dorsey. From watching and listening to a great variety of people, Joe learned what to do and what not to do. "In general in singing, it behooves you to do as few gestures as possible to distract from the singing, especially if you're singing well," he said.[3] When he sang on radio, broadcasting with bands from Chicago, he concentrated on his sound. Nobody could see him. He had to do his entire job by reaching people's ears.

Sifting through theories about the history of jazz singing, he came to his own conclusions. "The first instrument was the human voice. Drums were probably the second," he said. "The Indians, when they were chanting, were singing. The shepherds in Spain singing gypsy songs were expressing their feelings. The produce man selling baskets of peaches had his call. That's part of folklore. The human voice has always been expressing itself. There's just human expression. Mostly, I think jazz singing is improvisation.

"There are noises around us all the time. I use them, I draw on them for improv. For example, I just heard a colored fellow somewhere in this room," he said one day in the dining room of a casino in Atlantic City where he was performing. "I heard him tell someone near us"—Williams sang on descending notes, as clear as a violin, as bright as a voice can be,

" 'I

        heard

            that.'"

Swingers and Crooners

He continued, "For the blacks the need to improvise was born when African slaves were told they had to speak the language of their masters. And they played games with the things that were taken so formally and seriously. Like the word 'evening.' E'nen. Eeenen. E'nen. Duke Ellington would write all these noises around us all the time. . . . Writers say jazz singing began with Louis Armstrong and Ethel Waters. But there were always improvisers."[4]

Williams learned timing and stagecraft from comedians who worked with him in Chicago clubs. Over the years, he kept adding to his repertoire to suit his virile, gentle sound. He usually softened and lightened his blues with humor. Joe's were the love songs—the ones with a ribald and risqué joie de vivre, the laments of betrayed lovers, the sensitive invitations to intimacy.

Reflecting on his decision to become a singer, and the nature of jazz singing, he said, "I always heard the music. I could have played an instrument as well as I sing, whatever one called to me. But singing isn't something you do. It's really more something that comes through you."[5] For many years, he made tapes of himself, and he listened to them later, criticizing or praising himself and coaching himself to do better. Sometimes he asked a friend who was a classically trained singer for advice, even for something as small as the best way to handle a vowel on a high note. In performances, he heard himself in harmony with his background. "Before the show, I listen to the orchestra to make sure the music is right. I'll get my part right later," he said.[6] He looked into the audiences and seemed to be singing directly to people. Certainly he was communicating with them. But his primary concern all his life was the group of musicians behind him. He sang to them.

He also reflected on the value of having traumas and problems in life. "I wonder if it isn't better to have had some of that, and beatings, and go on to be recognized all over the world as a supertalent, a gifted person. I wonder if that was part of [Ethel Water's] talent, and if she put some of those experiences into her work." He murmured, "Anything but an ordinary life. Some people go through life without any real sunshine or storm. And she did have them and was able to express them. . . . The thing about experiences is you learn from them and know what to avoid."[7]

At forty-two, he married his fourth wife (with whom he continues to live happily) and decided to leave Basie and go out on his own. He wanted to sing more ballads. "When one grows up, it is time to leave home," he explained.[8] He had received great exposure on television and in the world's best concert houses with Basie. The recordings they made in 1956—"Roll 'em Pete," "Smack Dab in the Middle," "Every Day," and "All Right, Okay, You Win,"—had launched him onto a secure financial platform. He knew that television was one of the most important forums he could have. So he lined up six months of advance bookings. Basie presented Joe onstage at his first post-Basie band engagement in Boston.

Joe committed himself to continued growth and challenges. "One could very easily become stagnant," he said. "I was one of the fortunate ones." He kept adding new songs to his repertoire. "I just sing. The phrasing comes from putting things together that make sense."[9]

One of the most succinct appraisals of his work came from John S. Wilson, a *New York Times* critic, in 1972. "Williams has grown slowly but steadily from the powerful blues singer he was . . . to an extremely perceptive and convincing singer of ballads and unusual pop songs and, eventually to a relaxed, witty and debonair monologist. . . . He has a personal warmth that communicates particularly well in a small room. . . . The blues he sang with Basie are still the strong backbone of his repertoire, but he has become so skillful . . . that he could bring a sparkle to any bit of musical dross."[10]

Joe Williams is and always was a large presence in stature and voice in the jazz world. In his late seventies, he sang a pretty ballad, "Here's to Life," which had become so popular that audiences at Carnegie Hall gave him a standing ovation, just as they had done years earlier for his blues singing with Count Basie.

Nat "King" Cole

In California in 1937, Nat Cole, a struggling young pianist, wanted to start his own big band, but club owners wouldn't take a chance on an unknown. So he played for five dollars a night in any little club that would hire him. One night the owner of the Sewanee Inn in Los Angeles asked him to form a quartet and play for seventy-five dollars a week. Nat said yes. He didn't know it, but he was about to start a trend of singers with small combos, a large force in the golden age for jazz singers.

Nat hired bassist Wesley Prince and guitarist Oscar Moore. The legend is that Nat hired a drummer, too, but only Wesley and Oscar showed up; the truth is that there wasn't enough room or money for a drummer, and Nat probably didn't hire one. He was always as smart as his bright, sly-looking eyes suggested. Once, when a tipsy customer asked Nat to sing, he answered, "No. I don't sound good."[11] The club owner ordered Nat to sing—or else. So Nat sang "Sweet Lorraine," the theme song of bandleader Jimmie Noone. Noone was one of Nat's favorite musicians in Chicago, where Nat grew up. The club owner put a tinsel crown on Nat's head and called him Nat "King" Cole. Nat reluctantly wore the crown for a few weeks, then managed to lose it.

Nat had to keep singing by audience demand, but he was so shy that he asked Wesley and Oscar to sing with him, sometimes in unison. Wesley named the group the King Cole Trio. The men worked out arrangements together, but Nat had the special voice. His baritone had a mesmerizing, masculine edge that stood out when he took a solo part. He was regarded as such a good pianist that many singers asked him to play for their rehearsals. When he coached them about their phrasing, he taught himself, too. His vocal style was based on his light and airy, swinging piano style.

Nat worked hard to find jobs for the trio in California. Then they traveled across the country in his old car to the 52nd Street clubs in New York. By day, he went to the Brill Building, which was filled with song publishers, and looked for new songs. In the afternoons, he would rehearse alone in dark, empty clubs. He loved new songs. He was so busy practicing that many important people heard him in one place or another. Singer and songwriter Johnny Mercer, who was working as a host for an NBC radio show, heard Nat in a club across the street from the Los Angeles studio. Mercer loved Nat's style.

Nat was not handsome. He had slanty eyes and a very wide mouth, and he wore his hair in a pompadour. But he was tall and slim, and when he sat catty-corner to his piano and looked straight out at the audience, a slight smile played on his lips. His eyes seemed to carry the message that he knew everything about life and love. His voice was a warm whisper of a romantic man of the world. He had a low-key style. But a rhythmic pulse made his songs sprint. His voice had depth, although it had less than a two octave range. His breathiness made his sound heady and tender. And he sang in tune with the greatest of ease.

Johnny Mercer, who was also a founder of Capitol, a new record company in the early 1940s, bought masters of recordings Nat had made for a tiny company. Capitol reissued two of the recordings, "Vom Vim Veedle" and "All For You." For the first time, the King Cole Trio had good distribution. Its recordings ranked in the pop charts. In 1943, the men recorded about a dozen songs for Capitol. One was a novelty song Nat had written himself, a fable about a monkey taking a ride on a buzzard's back and urging the big bird to "Straighten Up and Fly Right." Nat had taken the idea from a sermon preached by his father, a Baptist minister. A nationwide hit, it went close to the top of the pop charts. Nat's new manager, Carlos Gastel, booked the trio to play in a Los Angeles theater as a warmup group for a big band. Critics preferred the trio to the band.

The King Cole Trio's seven years of struggle ended. Gradually, Nat's voice took the obvious lead. In 1946, he recorded "The Christmas Song," which became the number one hit in the country. Nat was persuaded to record with strings for this song. A few months later, he recorded the romantic ballad "I Love You for Sentimental Reasons." That too became a major hit. Nat then recorded Christmas songs for children, and they were also big sellers.

In 1947, Nat wanted to record a strange, moody tune called "Nature Boy," about a young wanderer who preached a message of universal love. Capitol's owners thought it was too odd. Nat finally persuaded them to put it out on the flip side of a pretty ballad, "Lost April." Within days of its release in May 1948, the disc jockeys were playing "Nature Boy" all the time. By June, "Lost April" was lost forever. "Nature Boy" was so popular that it became part of the folklore of the country. Nat joked that he was looking for a song called "Nature Girl." And when he rode through the countryside, he closed his eyes, he said, so he wouldn't have to look at nature.

Two years later, Capitol's owners asked Nat to record a tune called "Mona Lisa." Nat didn't think a song about the woman in the famous painting by Leonardo da Vinci would interest his fans. He was shocked when "Mona Lisa" became one of the best-selling records of his career. (Only one song, "Rambling Rose," recorded by Nat in 1962, may have topped "Mona Lisa.")

The King Cole Trio went through changes. It became Nat King Cole and His Trio. The personnel changed several times. Nat was the whole show. He didn't always play the piano in performances anymore. Instead he stood up at the microphone and hired accompanists. Studio orchestras played for recording sessions.

In his personal life, he went through turmoil. As he rose to become one of the world's most popular singers, his first marriage to a dancer ten years older than he ended in divorce. He then married a smart, glamorous young woman named Maria. She had done a little singing with Duke Ellington's band, and she helped Nat with his wardrobe, his diction, his skin care (all that greasy stage makeup), and even his career management decisions. Nat had been splitting the earnings from the King Cole Trio three ways equally. Maria reorganized the system so that he earned all the money and put his sidemen on salaries. They were very good salaries, to be sure, with huge Christmas bonuses.

Nat and Maria bought a brick mansion in fashionable Hancock Park in 1948, when it was an all-white, all-Christian section of Los Angeles. Neighbors protested and signed a petition asking him not to move in. At a meeting, they told him they didn't want any undesirable people in the neighborhood. He said, "Neither do I. If I see anyone undesirable coming in, I'll be the first to complain."[12] After the Coles moved in, someone fired a shotgun pellet through a window. No one was hurt. Eventually, the furor died down, and the Coles lived there in peace. They had children who played with neighborhood kids. And Nat and Maria gave parties attended by all their celebrity friends. But none of their neighbors befriended them or attended the parties. Years later, Hancock Park became completely integrated. An African-American mayor of Los Angeles lived there.

Natalie Cole, born in 1950, showed talent right away. Billy May, an arranger who worked with Cole on recordings and on tours, would always remember a day when Nat brought young Natalie to the May house. "He told her to sing for us," May said. Natalie, who was nicknamed "Sweetie," imitated Nat singing one of his hits at that time, "Walking My Baby Back Home." She sang with the spirit and charm of a little trooper at center stage. Then she suddenly stopped and said, "I have to go to the bathroom!"[13] She had a glow, an indefinable star quality, and she looked just like Nat, with her dark complexion and generous, large features.

Nat's life never seemed to get easier. The Internal Revenue Service was alerted by newspaper stories to the high cost of his wedding to Maria. The government investigated his finances and discovered he owed a tremendous amount in back taxes. No one in his business organization had paid them. Capitol Records and a bank made an arrangement that helped him pay the money out of his earnings. Maria put Nat on an allowance for years, until the debt was wiped out.

Then in 1956, he was attacked onstage by right-wing white extremists from a small town in Alabama, where he performed in an integrated group. (Nat had been born in Alabama and moved as a baby to Chicago.) The men leaped onstage and pushed him backward on the piano bench. He twisted his ankle. Police rushed to help Cole right away. More frightened than hurt, he said, "I love show business, but I don't want to die for it."[14] He left the tour for a while. When he rejoined it, in another state, he was criticized for performing for segregated audiences and for not taking a militant position in the civil rights movement.

The criticism wasn't fair. Everyone performed for segregated audiences in the South in those days. Nat believed he was advancing the cause of brotherhood simply by entertaining audiences of all races. Disgusted by segregation in Las Vegas casinos that prevented him from using all the facilities in places where his trio worked, Nat had insisted his contracts include equal rights. One casino owner backed him. So Nat paved the way for all African-American entertainers to enjoy equal rights in Las Vegas.

He often stood up for his rights alone. He once sued a hotel in the Midwest, and won, after the hotel didn't allow him to occupy rooms he had reserved. Another time, a white friend recalled sitting stubbornly with Nat very late at night in a hotel lobby in New York until the management stopped stalling and took him to his room. Nat then participated more frequently in organized civil rights actions involving entertainers. And he joined the NAACP, for which he had often performed benefits anyway.

In 1956, he became the first African-American entertainer to have his own network television show, on NBC. Then he discovered that he couldn't attract sponsors because of his race. NBC paid twenty thousand dollars a week to sustain the show. Nat accepted a much lower salary than he could have earned from doing club dates and concerts. But he persisted for a year. His television show attracted very large audiences. He kept having hit records in the 1940s and 1950s. "He never bragged," one friend recalled. Songwriters pushed their songs under hotel doors to him. They handed tunes to him in restaurants. Nat was always willing to take a look at a new song.

He believed his great success came from his storytelling talent. "I'm an interpreter of stories," he said. "And when I perform it's like I'm sitting down at my piano and telling fairy stories."[15] He never completely understood why people fell so in love with the sound of his warm voice. But his recording of "Unforgettable" came to be as much about the dreamy, hypnotic sound of his voice as it was a love song.

Because of the stresses of his life, he smoked constantly. In late 1964, he became ill with lung cancer. In February 1965, he died at age forty-eight. Toward the end of his life, he was beginning to feel the competition from a new style of popular singing: rock 'n' roll singers were taking over in the pop music world. Rock 'n' roll was obviously the coming thing. Nat hadn't liked the simpler harmonies and more aggressive, repetitive beat very well, and he had tried to stick to his usual repertoire of love songs for sophisticated audiences.

Since he was already legendary by the 1960s, it isn't likely his career would have lost its luster if he had survived to compete with rock 'n' roll. Jazz and jazz-influenced singers who established themselves as stars on their own by the 1950s were usually able to keep working in prestigious and glamorous places. But even for Nat, times had changed. His friends told of the day he called Capitol Records and heard the operator say, "Capitol Records, Home of the Beatles." He became very angry, for he had been one of Capitol's most important stars for years.

Hundreds of jazz and jazz-influenced singers successfully made the transition from decorations and sidepeople for the big bands to solo stars in the studios and on recordings. Some have already been mentioned, such as Frank Sinatra. Doris Day became far better known as a Hollywood star, singing in romantic musical comedies, than she had ever been as a big-band singer. Other important popular singers in the 1950s were Peggy Lee, Perry Como, Tony Bennett, Frankie Lane, Tony Martin, Rosemary Clooney, Kay Starr, and Dinah Shore.

Rosemary Clooney, with her earthy, sultry voice and her excellent timing and intonation, distinguished herself increasingly as the years went on. She started as a band singer with Tony Pastor. With her lovely voice and sense of humor, she made the simple novelty tune, "Come On-a My House," into a major hit in 1950. Later she sang with Duke

Ellington's band and worked with other great jazz musicians. The quality of her voice endured into the 1990s, despite its broadened vibrato.

Dinah Shore became a radio singing star first, then graduated to television, and for many years reigned as one of the country's favorite female singers of pop songs. As a pop performer, she sang with more of a country and western feeling than a jazz swing. She had a smooth, soft voice and a drawled, honeyed style of delivering lyrics.

Like Nat King Cole, Dinah became a superstar in the 1950s. Unlike Nat, she was white, and she had an easy time finding sponsors for her broadcasts. Similarly, Perry Como, a follower of Bing Crosby and regarded as one of the best singers in the country, became a much bigger star on radio and then television than he had been in the big-band era. Back when Nat had failed to find television sponsors, he predicted the time would come when African-Americans would overcome such obstacles. Today, when sponsors stand in line for popular shows featuring African-Americans, it's hard to imagine that the problem ever existed.

Carmen McRae

Another singer who struggled throughout the big-band era and later became a star was Carmen McRae. Her idol was Billie Holiday, from whom she learned the importance of telling a story with the music and lyrics. Carmen earned little fees as a pianist and singer in out-of-the-way clubs during the 1940s and early 1950s. She watched her girlfriend Sarah Vaughan become very popular in those days.

Carmen did a little singing with bands led by Benny Carter, Count Basie, and Mercer Ellington, Duke's son, but by the late 1940s, her career hadn't caught fire. Divorced from her first husband, Kenny Clarke, a revolutionary bebop drummer, she moved from New York to Chicago with a boyfriend. That relationship didn't work out. So she

120

Carmen McRae became revered for her impeccable storytelling abilities, which she claimed to have learned from Billie Holiday.

sought refuge with a girlfriend with whom she had worked as a chorus girl at Club Harlem, a popular African-American all-night hangout in Atlantic City. Carmen's friend helped her find a job as a singer-pianist in a club on Chicago's South Side, where Carmen developed her repertoire and style. She moved home to New York, where she worked in an office by day and sang and played piano in a Brooklyn club called the Bandbox at night.

There she met an excellent Dutch accordionist, Mat Mathews, who included her in a record date for the small new Stardust label. The label's owner fell in love with Carmen's clear, feminine voice and made more recordings with her. Her recordings circulated among musicians and may have helped to land her a regular job at Minton's Playhouse, where the beboppers had developed their style. There, the house bandleader, clarinetist Tony Scott, urged her to get up from the piano bench and sing at a microphone. She was terrified; she didn't know what to do with her hands. But she forced herself to try. Sure enough, she attracted attention. She recorded for the little Bethlehem label, then for Decca. Her recordings became popular. She was booked to appear in a Carnegie Hall concert with leading jazz musicians and singers.

While she was touring in Canada in 1954, the news reached her that she had won a popularity poll in *Down Beat* magazine. "I was thrilled," she recalled.[16] She began to appear in such nationally known clubs as Basin Street in New York. Soon she found herself in a position of prestige nearly comparable to Sarah Vaughan's. In 1955, Carmen was given *Metronome* magazine's Singer of the Year award.

She was still very pretty and youthful looking. There was a hint of the exotic in her manner, expression, and chiseled features. But Carmen was actually thirty-five years old by the time she achieved stardom. The closest she came to having a million-selling record was with "Skyliner." With that song and a very varied, hip repertoire including compositions from the great bebop pianist Thelonious Monk,

Broadway theater composers, and anyone else whose songs intrigued her, Carmen attracted fans who remained loyal to her. Some jazz critics called her the greatest jazz singer in the world.

Ella Fitzgerald became known for having rhythmic mastery. Sarah Vaughan's fame came to her first and foremost for her heavenly voice. Carmen's strength lay in her gift as a storyteller. Her voice was actually a little rough by the time she became famous, but her interpretive abilities had gained depth and power from her years of experience and commitment to lyrics and music. Her understanding of harmonies had their roots in the lessons she had learned from her first days of enchantment by the embellishments of bebop.

Respiratory illness forced Carmen to retire in 1992. Protégés such as Helen Merrill and Carol Sloane, who developed in the 1960s, a musical generation after Carmen, called her the "professor." Vanessa Rubin, a singer who emerged as a promising star in the 1990s, worshipped Carmen's ability to interpret the lyrics of songs and make audiences listen raptly to every word. Early in 1994, Rubin released an album on the RCA Novus label that was billed as a tribute to Carmen. "I want Carmen to know how much she is revered," Vanessa explained.[17] Carmen McRae died on November 11, 1994.

Mel Tormé began singing professionally as a child in the African-American neighborhood where he grew up in Chicago. He played with big bands, but he became better known as a crooner with his own group, the Melltones, and as a singer in movies and clubs. He became one of the most important jazz singers of the century and a leader of his own groups of all sizes.

Some of the singers, who became successful during the big-band era and enhanced their stardom during the golden age of singers in the 1950s, showed great generosity to newcomers. When Pearl Bailey heard Tony Bennett during an audition at a New York club, she shouted to the club owner, "Hire that kid."[18] Billy Eckstine encouraged Tony as well, and advised him on how to improve his singing.

Mel Tormé, shown here in 1948, began singing professionally as a child in Chicago in the 1930s. He was blessed with a soft, intimate voice and acquired perfect technique.

Tony Bennett's vitality and joie de vivre made him a very popular jazz-influenced singer beginning in the 1950s.

Simply by listening to stars who came before them, many singers learned their craft. In the 1950s, a young pianist and singer, Nina Simone, forged her style by blending jazz, pop, and gospel-rooted music. Her reedy voice and intensity made her a charismatic star by the 1960s. Similarly, Vic Damone, under the influence of Crosby and his disciples, became a popular singer of romantic ballads in the 1950s. And countless young singers listened to Nat Cole.

A great star to emerge from Cole's shadow was rhythm-and-blues singer Ray Charles. Ray committed himself to singing in Nat's style for a long time, before his own unique, swinging, soulful style emerged.[19] He became a legendary singer in the rock 'n' roll and rhythm and blues revolution that eclipsed jazz singing commercially by the late 1960s.

Chapter Eight The Decline, Fall, and Rebirth of Jazz Singing

For several reasons, jazz singing ceased to interest young people in the 1960s. Jazz instrumentalists began trying to take the innovations of bebop further. Instead of improvising on the chords of written songs, or composing new, melodic songs based on the chords of old tunes, they used modes and foreign scales to inspire compositions. The music became more complex. General audiences were puzzled by the modernity.

Still other musicians simply played any notes that came into their heads, at rhythms that seemed random, and their music sounded cacophonous and even atonal. The experimental music drove people out of the jazz clubs. Jazz musicians and singers playing familiar old styles of jazz had few places to perform.

At the same time, young people were changing radically. The United States had become a prosperous country after World War II. With more money and educational opportunities, many young people didn't have to struggle for survival, and could choose what they wanted to do with their lives. The country elected a handsome, young, idealistic president, John F. Kennedy, who tried to bring a bright vision of the future to the world. One of his new programs, the Peace Corps, sent young Americans with technological expertise and compassion for others to live and teach in the villages of impoverished Third World countries. At home, folk music celebrating the joys of the simple life and the dignity of the common man became popular with young people.

Then President Kennedy was assassinated in 1963. The country went into shock and mourning. Lyndon Baines Johnson moved into the White House; he was a masterful politician who knew exactly how to get Congress to approve socially progressive laws for the country. Johnson had been in Washington a long time and knew secrets about members of Congress. They didn't want to be exposed. So Congress passed civil rights and equal opportunity acts for African-Americans and other minority groups, women, people with disabilities, and the elderly.

Along with all the good President Johnson did the for country with his "Great Society" social programs, his policy of escalating the civil war in Vietnam wreaked havoc. Americans divided into two camps: supporters of the war, who believed it was being fought to preserve democracy, and opponents, who didn't trust the government's policy.

Young people, who had been shocked by Kennedy's death, became angry and cynical. As one form of protest against violence in the United States and the war abroad, they turned to loud popular music with simple harmonies and an elemental beat. Young singers wrote their own tunes, which reflected their experiences and beliefs. African-Americans set their life stories to highly amplified, gospel-inspired music. And some jazz musicians insisted upon exploring their rebellious experiments for artistic and political reasons.

Saxophonist Stan Getz was one of the few jazz musicians who managed to keep jazz before the public and stay on the cutting edge of popular music. He did it by introducing the refreshing, peaceful sound of Brazilian music and Brazilian singers and instrumentalists. Antonio Carlos

Swingers and Crooners

Jobim, Joao Gilberto, and Astrud Gilberto became familiar singers for North American audiences.

Trumpeter Miles Davis rejuvenated American jazz by blending his eerie, haunting sound with electric instruments. His invention, called fusion jazz, attracted fans among youngsters who could no longer react emotionally to the soft sounds of pure, classic, acoustic jazz.

Why could listeners no longer accept that sound? Simply put, public events had become too violent. Reverend Martin Luther King Jr. and Senator Robert Kennedy were assassinated in 1968. Less respected for his ideas at the time but also a tragic figure, Governor George Wallace was shot and crippled by a would-be assassin while running for president. These were troubled times, and they were "a-changing," as folk-singing superstar Bob Dylan chanted. It seemed as if young people were using high-decibel music to block out and escape from the horror of public events; jazz musicians were reflecting the chaos in their own way.

When the administration of President Richard M. Nixon was exposed as corrupt in the 1970s, the revelation did nothing to ease the country's tensions. Music got even louder at rock concerts and in discotheques, where people went to dance uninhibitedly. In all these places, young people smoked marijuana with its strong, heady, pungent smell. That was the least powerful of the drugs that became epidemic in the country.

Against the background of calamitous events and the music that accompanied them, jazz singers with their characteristic, soft, intimate sounds didn't have much chance of attracting attention. Singer Helen Merrill had toured with Earl Hines, then in 1954 recorded the album *Helen Merrill*, with great jazz musicians playing old songs arranged by Quincy Jones. She even included "Don't Explain," a Billie Holiday composition. But Helen couldn't find enough work to support herself; her jazz singing style was advanced, informed by bebop with the written notes frequently a half-tone away from what she was singing. In the 1960s, she packed up and went to Europe.

For the next two decades, she lived in Italy and France, working with the best American and European musicians she could find. Many American musicians had moved to Europe because they couldn't find jazz jobs in the United States. Helen became well known and even had her own television show in Italy. Invited to perform in Japan, she repeated her singing success and, as a disc jockey, had her own English-language radio show on the Far East Network.

Carol Sloane, Mark Murphy, Jackie Paris, Anne Marie Moss, and many other fine jazz singers, who had established themselves commercially in the 1940s and 1950s, struggled to survive during the 1960s and 1970s. Even Jon Hendricks, who was successful with his trio in the United States, had to sing in England for a while to support his family. Cab Calloway, who had given up his band in 1947, became the toast of Broadway in 1950 with his role as "Sportin' Life" in *Porgy and Bess*. After that, to earn a living, he had to play intermission music for Harlem Globetrotters basketball games. In 1967, he had another Broadway hit in *Hello, Dolly*, with singer Pearl Bailey. He had helped her earlier in her career; she returned the favor when he really needed it.

Tony Bennett and other singers slipped into obscurity. Dominating pop music were singers who shouted and wailed in groups with an elemental beat. Without sophistication or subtlety, they pounded away on their instruments. The jazz world was dominated by a small group of avant-garde musicians and singers whose experimental music was dubbed "free jazz." Few people had the patience or interest to listen to it.

But in the midst of all these changes, a renaissance in jazz was brewing. It began in the late 1960s, when the National Endowment for the Arts recognized jazz as an art form and began funding projects. Music schools and liberal arts colleges set up jazz programs, where musicians became teachers. Throughout the 1970s, hidden from the public, youngsters studied jazz formally, learning excellent techniques from the founders of the art. Classical music teachers taught young jazz musicians in schools, too.

By 1980, young jazz instrumentalists were getting chances to perform with the old masters of jazz in clubs and concerts. And as the old masters died, young protégés took their place. Also, rock 'n' roll had lost some of its advantage in the marketplace, because rock concerts had become dangerous places—fights broke out, and audience members were injured.

Swingers and Crooners

Teenagers turned to other forms of entertainment, especially videos. But older people sought a new form of entertainment. So record companies opened their vaults filled with classic jazz recordings, reissued them, and discovered that adults were eager to buy them. That's when Columbia decided to take a chance on trumpeter Wynton Marsalis, and then other young lions of jazz. These new recordings sold, too.

A technological advance—the mass marketing of music on compact discs—gave the public's interest in jazz a special shot in the arm. Young people, who were dubbed "yuppies" by the media, could afford to buy sleek, expensive electronic equipment, including CD players, as status symbols. They discovered they liked jazz, and they began to show up for performances led by young jazz players.

Unfortunately, new young singers were left out. Nobody was paying attention to them. The great old singers—Ella, Sarah, Carmen, Anita, Joe Williams, Mel Tormé, Jon Hendricks, and Frank Sinatra—were still performing in grand style. Tony Bennett was virtually rediscovered to become a star all over again. Betty Carter became more prominent.

Betty, who had begun her career in the swing era, was really one of a kind. Throughout the years, she had persisted as an eccentric, creative jazz singer, performing her own compositions and recording herself for her own Bet-Car label when major commercial labels feared to take a chance with her. She was an iconoclastic singer; she pulled apart the old songs note by note and then put them back together again, often in ways that made them barely recognizable. She could take a song like "My Favorite Things" and make it swing at breakneck speed. Just as often, she liked to sing songs with odd names, weird harmonies, and complex, constantly changing tempos.

Alone among the singers, after many lean years of struggle and persistence, she had made free jazz singing commercially viable. She had the charisma, style, and experience to fill a jazz club or concert hall and excite audiences made up of people with both avant-garde and traditional tastes. When other singers tried her ideas, nobody showed up. Following in Betty's footsteps, singer Janet Lawson, for example, with an exquisite soprano

130

voice, made an album and won a Grammy nomination in the early 1980s. But Janet sang only her own improvisations, and her audiences were small.

In New York City, Susannah McCorkle began attracting fans. She had studied Billie Holiday recordings religiously. Bobby McFerrin, who became known for his incandescent scat singing and nature sounds, also came into vogue. A vocal magician, he could sound like a trumpet and a string bass, changing instrument sounds within a fraction of a second, and all the while playing percussion by tapping his own chest. He emulated the eerie sound of a trumpet for the sound track of the 1986 film *Round Midnight*, starring saxophonist Dexter Gordon. McFerrin also began winning Grammys and jazz singing polls. And his own composition "Don't Worry, Be Happy" became an international hit.

Al Jarreau, who could sing up-tempo songs with great excitement, became the other best-known new jazz singing star of the 1980s. There were no women with equally fresh, exciting styles and sounds. Then along came Cassandra Wilson, a young vocalist from Jackson, Mississippi, who had done some traditional singing and guitar playing at home with her father. One of the first things she did when she moved to New York City was to discover Betty Carter. Cassandra sang with a rich contralto that sometimes reminded people of Sarah Vaughan.

When Cassandra recorded an album of standards, including the antique Irving Berlin song "Blue Skies," she caused a great deal of excitement. Her voice was rich, and her harmonic ideas were very affecting. Gone was the sentimentality and romance of the original tune. Instead, she communicated a modern conception of love as a complex, sometimes awkward, dissonant arrangement. The public was ready for experimental music. Cassandra established herself as the most interesting young female jazz singer around.

Seemingly out of nowhere came a young, blind jazz singer, Diane Schuur, who could sing the blues, ballads, and up-tempo songs in a shrill, exciting style. She electrified an audience at Carnegie Hall in the late 1980s. Her albums began selling well, and she worked in very prominent halls.

Other traditional singers, Judy Niemack, Roseanna Vitro, Carmen Lundy, and Carla White among them, made albums and appeared in

Cassandra Wilson fell in love with Betty Carter's style and followed in her footsteps.

clubs. Another singer, Dee Dee Bridgewater, who liked to experiment, tried the old trick of going to Paris to acquire glamour and become successful. Niemack, who began with classical training at the New England Conservatory in Boston, built a career both in Europe and the United States as an improvisational jazz and pop singer praised by critics. But no matter how good they were at singing in classic jazz styles, young singers had a very hard time convincing club owners and concert producers to pay attention. It was as if the tables had been turned. Instrumentalists were back in vogue. Most singers were treated as afterthoughts.

By the mid-1980s, though, young critics, who weren't afraid to say that the emperor had no clothes, began to tell it the way it really was. It was painful for loyal old fans. An aging Ella Fitzgerald was losing control of her voice. Finally, she became too sick to perform. Sarah Vaughan suddenly died in 1990. Carmen McRae carried on for only two more years. Anita O'Day lost her ability to sing well. Lena Horne had done a great one-person show on Broadway in 1982, but her voice became a bit wobbly in the mid-1990s. Chris Connor, who had made a comeback in the 1980s, with the renaissance of interest in jazz, still sounded vital and exciting. But one jazz singer is not enough to carry on a tradition.

Record companies began signing talented young singers in the 1990s, hoping to replace the great stars of the past. Among the newcomers was Jeanie Bryson, Dizzy Gillespie's daughter (by a woman other than his beloved wife). Vanessa Rubin, who had performed throughout the 1980s in small clubs, working by day as a teacher, signed a contract with RCA Novus in the 1990s, and her career gained momentum.

Columbia gave its handsome young recording artist Harry Connick Jr., a pianist, singer, and friend of Wynton Marsalis, the chance to make a vocal album. He went into New York's Algonquin Hotel as a supper club entertainer. The critics discovered his enormous energy, wit, and talent. He went on to record "It Had to Be You" for the soundtrack of the movie *When Harry Met Sally*. It wasn't long before he was hailed as a new Sinatra, and he began a career as a movie actor, too.

Because he had been brought up in the home of swing era-rooted guitarist Bucky Pizzarelli, young John Pizzarelli Jr. found it natural to start a career as a singer and guitarist himself. First he performed with his father. Then he went out with his own trio, including his bass-playing brother, and concentrated on reanimating Nat King Cole tunes from the 1930s and 1940s. Pizzarelli's group has been in demand in the 1990s.

Columbia also signed Nnenna (pronounced Nina) Freelon in hopes of discovering a new Sarah Vaughan. By the mid-1990s, she was ranking high in popularity polls. So was Diane Reeves. The Concord label signed several young singers. Blue Note backed Kurt Elling, who sings in the bebop-rooted tradition.

The most startling discovery of all in the 1990s was a man in his thirties from Kansas City named Kevin Mahogany, whose body seemed larger than life, and whose robust baritone voice made a similar impression. He had college degrees in music and spent years gigging in clubs, primarily in Kansas City and the Midwest. Booked to play in a Chicago jazz club, he was asked if he would let vibes player Gust Tsilis join his group. Kevin said he would be delighted to welcome the man, whom he had never met but whose reputation he respected. Tsilis also happened to work for Enja, an excellent European recording label. He loved Kevin's voice and introduced Kevin to Enja's owner. Kevin signed a recording contract. Then his rich voice and versatility began to circulate in the right jazz circles. He was soon performing all around the country and—especially important for him—in the most prominent places in the Big Apple. Wynton Marsalis chose him to be the new Lincoln Center Jazz Orchestra's official vocalist.

Kevin had listened to every old recording he could find. He found himself compared to Billy Eckstine and Joe Williams. He admired Williams and borrowed liberally from his repertoire; he had the ability to do this and still stand up to the comparison. The 1990s was tentatively emerging as a new golden age of singers, or at least an age of fresh opportunities. The art of jazz singing, it has become clear, is not going to die.

There are so many singers worthy of mention that one book cannot possibly contain them all. Following are ten of those worth noting:

1. Chet Baker, who made his career as a trumpeter, was also a great, atmospheric singer; his recordings are widely available.

His recording of "My Funny Valentine" was one of his hits.

2. George Benson, a pop singer and guitarist, began as a jazz musician.

3. Dizzy Gillespie, in addition to playing trumpet, recorded creative, improvised vocal performances with singer Joe Carroll.

4. Johnny Hartman had one of the most beautiful baritones in jazz. Many of his recordings are classics, such as his version of the song "Lush Life" with John Coltrane.

5. Bill Henderson, an interesting stylist, was one of Sarah Vaughan's favorite singers.

6. Michele Hendricks, the daughter of Jon Hendricks, has albums of her own on the Muse label.

7. Diana Krall, a newcomer in the 1990s, records for GRP.

8. Cleo Laine, a British-born singer, has done many fine albums.

9. Weslia Whitfield, a classically-trained soprano, started in the chorus of the San Francisco Opera, then took a left turn into jazz-influenced singing of classic American popular songs. She has risen steadily over the years, recently becoming a star in the Algonquin Hotel and concert halls. When she was shot during a fight between two strangers on the street in San Francisco, she was paralyzed from the waist down, but she has never let her disability interfere with her career. She has recordings on the Landmark label .

10. Leo Watson was a great scatter who had a brief, zany career in the 1930s and 1940s. His recordings are difficult to find but worthwhile for their wit and improvisation.

Source Notes

Chapter Two

Remarks by the musicians Danny Barker, Dave Frishberg, and Arvel Shaw were made directly to the author in interviews.

1 Terms such as "black and tan," "good-timing," and "Blue Monday" are often used by jazz historians, who use the authentic language of early jazz, blues, and gospel musicians.

2 Gary Giddins, *Satchmo* (New York: A Dolphin Book, Doubleday, 1988), p. 26.

3 Ibid., p. 51.

4 Richard Meryman, editor, *Louis Armstrong: A Self Portrait* (New York: Eakins Press, 1971). The quotation can be found in Leslie Gourse, *Louis' Children: American Jazz Singers* (New York: William Morrow and Co., 1984), p. 29.

5 Leslie Gourse, *Louis' Children*, p. 30.

Chapter Three

1 Leslie Gourse, *Louis' Children: American Jazz Singers* (New York: William Morrow and Co., 1984), p. 33.

2 From a personal interview by the author with Mel Tormé in 1982. The quotation can be found in Leslie Gourse, *Louis' Children*, p. 192.

Chapter Five

1 John Chilton, *Billie's Blues* (New York: Da Capo Press, 1975), p. 43.

2 John Chilton, *Billie's Blues*, p. 19.

3 Leslie Gourse, *Louis' Children: American Jazz Singers* (New York: William Morrow and Co., 1984), p. 85.

4 Billie Holiday with William Dufty, *Lady Sings the Blues* (New York: Viking Penguin, 1984; originally published by Doubleday and Co., 1956), p. 74.

5 Helen Forrest and Bill Libby, *I Had the Craziest Dream* (New York: Coward, McCann & Geoghegan, 1981). The quotation can be found in Leslie Gourse, *Louis' Children*, p. 107.

6 Robert O'Meally, *Lady Day: The Many Faces of Billie Holiday* (New York: Arcade Publishing, 1991), p. 130.

7 Billie Holiday with William Dufty, *Lady Sings the Blues*, p. 116.

8 Leslie Gourse, *Louis' Children*, p. 96.

9 Leslie Gourse, *Louis' Children*, p. 83.

10 Stuart Nicholson, *Ella Fitzgerald: A Biography of the First Lady of Jazz* (New York: Charles Scribner's Sons, 1994), p. 122 and other pages.

11 Leslie Gourse, "Celebrating Ella!" *Jazz Times* (September 1991), p. 17.

12 Leslie Gourse, *Louis' Children*, p. 114.

13 Leslie Gourse, *Louis' Children*, p. 113.

14 George T. Simon, *The Big Bands*, 4th ed. (New York: Schirmer Books, 1981) pp. 265–266.

15 George T. Simon, *The Big Bands*, p. 166.

16 Interview by author with Sparky Tavares, valet and road companion to Nat "King" Cole.

17 Leslie Gourse, *Louis' Children*, p. 243.

18 Whitney Balliett Jr., review of a concert at Carnegie Hall, New York, *The New Yorker* (September 1982).

19 "AMC Great Movie Classics," a short, explanatory narrative about Hollywood history broadcast on the American Movie Classics cable channel between films in 1995.

20 Leslie Gourse, *Louis' Children*, p. 108.

21 Leslie Gourse, *Louis' Children*, p. 110.

22 Bobby Short, in a lecture about Ivie Anderson delivered at St. Peter's Lutheran Church at Citicorp, New York, 1982.

23 Anita O'Day and George Eels, *High Times, Hard Times* (New York: G. P. Putnam's Sons, 1981).

24 Leslie Gourse, *Louis' Children*, p. 236.

Chapter Six

1 Leslie Gourse, *Louis' Children: American Jazz Singers* (New York: William Morrow and Co., 1984), p. 136.

2 As told on Marian McPartland's "Piano Jazz" radio show in 1986. The quotation can be found in Leslie Gourse, *Sassy: The Life of Sarah Vaughan* (New York: Charles Scribner's Sons, 1993), p. 18.

3 Stanley Dance, *The World of Earl Hines* (New York: Da Capo Books, 1977). The quotation can be found in Leslie Gourse, *Sassy*, p. 19.

4 Leslie Gourse, *Sassy*, p. 25.

5 Interview by author with Robert Richards, an illustrator and close friend of Sarah Vaughan.

6 Leslie Gourse, *Sassy*, p. 47.

7 Leslie Gourse, *Sassy*, p. 77.

8 Leslie Gourse, *Sassy*, p. 232.

9 Leslie Gourse, *Louis' Children*, p. 169.

Chapter Seven

1 Leslie Gourse, *Every Day: The Story of Joe Williams* (London: Quartet Books, 1985), p. 34.

2 Leslie Gourse, *Every Day*, p. 175.

3 Leslie Gourse, *Louis' Children: American Jazz Singers* (New York: William Morrow and Co., 1984), p. 216.

4 Leslie Gourse, *Louis' Children*, p. 221.

5 Leslie Gourse, *Louis' Children*, p. 212.

6 Leslie Gourse, *Louis' Children*, p. 213.

7 Leslie Gourse, *Louis' Children*, p. 215.

8 Leslie Gourse, *Louis' Children*, p. 219.

9 Leslie Gourse, *Louis' Children*, p. 223.

10 John Wilson, review of Joe Williams, *New York Times*, 1974.

11 Leslie Gourse, *Unforgettable: The Life and Mystique of Nat King Cole* (New York: St. Martin's Press, 1991), p. 33.

12 Leslie Gourse, *Unforgettable*, p. 104.

13 Leslie Gourse, *Unforgettable*, p. 162.

14 Leslie Gourse, *Unforgettable*, p. 177.

15 Leslie Gourse, *Louis' Children*, p. 196.

16 Interview by author with Carmen McRae, 1993.

17 Interview by author with Vanessa Rubin, 1994.

18 Leslie Gourse, *Louis' Children*, p. 297.

19 Ray Charles and David Ritz, *Brother Ray* (New York: Warner Books, 1978), p. 56.

Suggested Listening

This list is based on the MUZE listings used in major music stores. Often the recordings for which singers became famous are no longer listed under their original titles, but they have been reissued under new titles or in boxed collections. The titles listed here are those available in 1996.

This list is in chronological order—that is, in the approximate order in which the artists emerged as stars.

Bessie Smith. *The Complete Recordings*, Vol. 1–5, Boxed Collections, Columbia/Legacy, 1991–1996.

Ethel Waters, *1925–26, 1926–30, 1929–31, 1932– 33, 1935–40*, all on the Classics label, 1992.

Louis Armstrong, *25 Greatest Hot Fives and Sevens*, Living Era, 1995; *Louis Armstrong and Earl Hines*, Vol. 4, Columbia; *Ella and Louis*, Verve, 1972.

Mildred Bailey, *The Rocking Chair Lady*, Decca, 1994.

Bing Crosby, *16 Most Requested Songs*, Columbia/Legacy, 1992. Note: The music store bins also contain CDs by singers such as Perry Como, Vic Damone, and Dick Haymes, who were directly influenced by Crosby, as well as by dancer Fred Astaire, who looked to Crosby for instructions about phrasing and interpretation in his singing, and Rosemary Clooney, who regard Bing as a role model.

Billie Holiday, *1933–37*, Classics label; *Billie Holiday and Her Orchestra*, 1937–39, Classics label; *Lady in Satin*, Columbia, 1958.

Ella Fitzgerald, *Harold Arlen Song Book*, Verve, 1961. (All the songbooks by Ella—music by George Gershwin, Duke Ellington, and Cole Porter—are on Verve, and all are superb.) Other greats include *Ella and Louis*, Verve,

1972 and *Ella Fitzgerald and Joe Pass*, Pablo, 1976. The bins are filled with recordings by Ella.

Sarah Vaughan, *with Clifford Brown*, Emarcy, 1954; *No Count Sarah*, Emarcy, 1958; *I Love Brazil*, Pablo, 1994; *The Complete Sarah Vaughan on Mercury*, Vols. 1–4, from the 1950s into the 1960s; *The Roulette Years*, 1960–1963. She won her only Grammy for an album of George Gershwin's music, with Michael Tilson Thomas, Columbia, 1981.

Frank Sinatra, *Come Fly With Me*, 1957, and *Come Dance With Me*, 1958, both on Capitol. The bins in music stores are filled with a huge, varied collection of recordings by Sinatra.

Anita O'Day, *Uptown*, with Roy Eldridge and Gene Krupa, Columbia.

Peggy Lee, with Benny Goodman, Columbia; *Fever and Other Hits*, DRG.

Jimmy Rushing, *Mr. Five by Five*, Topaz Jazz, 1996; *The Essential Jimmy Rushing*, Vanguard.

Mel Tormé, *16 Most Requested Songs*, Legacy, 1993; *Best of Mel Tormé*, Curb Records, 1993.

Carmen McRae, *Carmen Sings Monk*, Novus; *For Lady Day*, Vols. 1 and 2, Novus, 1995. Also see Betty Carter below.

Billy Eckstine, *Jazz Masters* 22, with many of his famous songs, including "My Foolish Heart" and "I Apologize," Verve, 1994. Eckstine is also included singing duets with Sarah Vaughan in her complete Mercury recordings.

Al Hibbler, *After the Lights Go Down Low*, Atlantic.

Tony Bennett, *16 Most Requested Songs*, Legacy; *Forty Years of Tony Bennett*, a boxed collection, Legacy, 1991.

Joe Williams, *Here's To Life*, Telarc, 1994; *Joe Williams Live*, Original Jazz Classics, 1973; *Count Basie, Joe Williams*, Compact Jazz, Verve, contains all of Joe's early hits with Basie.

Nat "King" Cole, several early trio recordings on Capitol; *Nat King Cole Sings, George Shearing Plays*, Capitol/EMI, 1962; *Nat King Cole at the Sands*, Capitol/EMI, 1960.

Chris Connor, *Lover, Come Back To Me*, Evidence, 1995.

June Christy, with Stan Kenton, *Road Show*, Capitol/EMI, 1959.

Dinah Washington, *Blue Gardenia: Songs of Love*, Emarcy, 1995; *The Complete Dinah Washington on Mercury*, Vols. 1–7, 1987; *What a Diff'rence A Day Makes*, Mercury, 1959.

Lambert, Hendricks and Ross, *Sing a Song of Basie*, GRP, 1972.

Eddie Jefferson, *The Jazz Singer*, Evidence. Several other recordings also include the song "Moody's Mood for Love."

Chet Baker, *Let's Get Lost: The Best of Chet Baker*, Blue Note, 1989.

Helen Merrill, *The Complete Helen Merrill on Mercury*, 1986.

Carol Sloane, *Sweet and Slow*, 1993, *When I Look In Your Eyes*, 1994, and others, all on Concord.

Bobby McFerrin, *Small Pleasures*, EMI, 1982, which includes "Don't Worry, Be Happy."

Al Jarreau, *Look to the Rainbow: Live in Europe*, Warner Brothers Records, 1977.

Betty Carter, with Ray Charles, DCC, 1961; with Carmen McRae, *Live at the Great American Music Hall*, Verve, 1988; *I'm Yours, You're Mine*, Verve, 1996.

Cassandra Wilson, *Blue Skies*, Verve.

Jeanie Bryson, *I Love Being Here with You*, Telarc, 1993; *Tonight I Need You So*, Telarc, 1994, includes "Honeysuckle Rose."

Harry Connick Jr., *When Harry Met Sally*, Columbia, 1989.

Diana Krall, *All for You*, Impulse, 1996; *Only Trust Your Heart*, GRP, 1995.

Kevin Mahogany, *Double Rainbow*, 1993, *Songs and Moments*, 1994, and *You Got What It Takes*, 1995, all on Enja; *Kevin Mahogany*, Warner Brothers, 1996.

139

For Further Reading

Music magazines often publish stories on classic and contemporary singers. Among the magazines that can be found on newsstands and in music libraries are *Down Beat*, *Jazz Times*, *Jazz Iz*, and *Musician*.

Albertson, Chris. *Bessie*. Lanham, Md.: Scarborough House, Madison Books, 1974.

Armstrong, Louis. *My Life in New Orleans*. Englewood Cliffs, N.J.: Prentice Hall, 1954. Reprinted by Da Capo Press, New York, 1986.

Balliett, Whitney. *American Singers*. New York: Oxford University Press, 1988.

Brown, Sandford. *Louis Armstrong: Swinging, Singing Satchmo*. New York: Franklin Watts, 1993.

Calloway, Cab, and Bryant Rollins. *Of Minnie the Moocher and Me*. New York: Thomas Y. Crowell Co., 1976.

Charles, Ray, and David Ritz. *Brother Ray*. New York: Warner Books, 1978.

Chilton, John. *Billie's Blues*. New York: Da Capo Press, 1975.

Clarke, Donald. *Wishing on the Moon: The Life and Times of Billie Holiday*. New York: Viking, 1994.

Clooney, Rosemary, and Raymond Strait. *This for Remembrance*. New York: Playboy Press Paperbacks, 1977–79.

Dahl, Linda. *Stormy Weather*. New York: Limelight Editions, 1989. A study of women jazz musicians and singers.

Dance, Stanley. *The World of Earl Hines*. New York: Da Capo Books, 1977.

Forrest, Helen, and Bill Libby. *I Had the Craziest Dream*. New York: Coward, McCann & Geoghegan, 1981.

Giddins, Gary. *Satchmo*. New York: A Dolphin Book, Doubleday, 1988.

Gourse, Leslie. *Billie Holiday: The Tragedy and Triumph of Lady Day*. Danbury, Conn.: Franklin Watts, 1995.

Gourse, Leslie. *Every Day: The Story of Joe Williams*. London: Quartet Books, 1985.

Gourse, Leslie. *Louis' Children: American Jazz Singers*. New York: William Morrow and Co., 1984.

Gourse, Leslie. *Sassy: The Life of Sarah Vaughan*. New York: Charles Scribner's Sons, 1993.

Gourse, Leslie. *Unforgettable: The Life and Mystique of Nat King Cole*. New York: St. Martin's Press, 1991.

Holiday, Billie, with William Dufty. *Lady Sings the Blues*. New York: Viking Penguin, 1984. Originally published by Doubleday and Co. in 1956.

Meryman, Richard, editor. *Louis Armstrong: A Self Portrait*. New York: Eakins Press, 1971.

Nicholson, Stuart. *Ella Fitzgerald: A Biography of the First Lady of Jazz*. New York: Charles Scribner's Sons, 1994.

O'Day, Anita, and George Eels. *High Times, Hard Times*. New York: G. P. Putnam's Sons, 1981.

O'Meally, Robert. *Lady Day: The Many Faces of Billie Holiday*. New York: Arcade Publishing, 1991.

Placksin, Sally. *American Women in Jazz*. New York: Wideview Books, 1982. Note: this book is soon to be reissued with updated materials.

Pleasants, Henry. *The Great American Popular Singers*. New York: Simon & Schuster, 1974.

Simon, George T. *The Big Bands*. 4th ed. New York: Schirmer Books, 1981.

Seymour, Gene. *Jazz: The Great American Art*. Danbury, Conn.: Franklin Watts, 1995.

Waters, Ethel. *His Eye Is on the Sparrow*. Westport, Conn.: Greenwood Press, 1978. Paperback reprint by Da Capo Books, New York, 1992.

Wyman, Carolyn. *Ella Fitzgerald: Jazz Singer Supreme*. New York: Franklin Watts, 1993.

Index

Page numbers in *italics* refer to photographs. Principal references to musicians appear in **boldface**.

Index

Swingers and Crooners